JIHAD, PEACE, AND INTER-COMMUNITY RELATIONS IN ISLAM

JIHAD, PEACE, AND INTER-COMMUNITY RELATIONS IN ISLAM

Maulana Wahiduddin Khan

Translated from Urdu and Edited by
Yoginder Sikand

Rupa & Co

Published 2010 by

Rupa & Co

7/16, Ansari Road, Daryaganj,
New Delhi 110 002

Sales Centres:

Allahabad Bengaluru Chandigarh Chennai
Hyderabad Jaipur Kathmandu
Kolkata Mumbai

Typeset by
Mindways Design
1410 Chiranjiv Tower
43 Nehru Place
New Delhi 110 019

Printed in India by
Rekha Printers Pvt Ltd.
A-102/1, Okhla Industrial Area, Phase-II,
New Delhi-110 020

Contents

Preface

Recent decades have witnessed the emergence of movements across the world in the name of religion, some of which are fuelled by a deep-rooted hatred for other faiths and their adherents. These include some self-styled 'Islamic' movements that see themselves as struggling against 'forces of falsehood' in order to establish an 'Islamic State' based on their understanding of the Divine law or *shariah*. Several of them are also engaged in armed struggles, which they regard as jihads. While some of these movements can be seen as responses or reactions to injustices suffered by Muslim communities in different parts of the world, many have deviated considerably from the path of Islam, as Islam does not permit terrorist activities. In this way, they have given Muslims and Islam a bad name. They have played no small role in contributing to the rapid spread of what is now called Islamophobia, with their fiery rhetoric against people of other faiths, whom they brand as 'enemies of Islam'. They are thus a major obstacle in the path of promoting better relations between Muslims and others, something that is of absolute necessity in today's 'global village'.

New Delhi-based Maulana Wahiduddin Khan is one of the few *ulama* or traditionally-trained Islamic scholars throughout the world to have made a deep and incisive study of the politics and ideology of extremist self-styled 'Islamic' groups and to have critiqued them from within an Islamic framework. By arguing that the politics and ideology of these groups are a deviation from Islamic teachings as he interprets them, he is able to articulate a very necessary Islamic critique of terrorism in the name of Islam. This is a crucial means to seek to convince Muslims that the purveyors of terror who speak in the name of Islam are actually doing their religion the greatest disservice.

I have had the wonderful opportunity of interacting with Maulana Wahiduddin Khan for over a decade now and of studying his major works. Two years ago, he was kind enough to gift me an entire set of his Urdu books, which number several dozens. This was after I evinced a desire to translate some of his writings on issues related to Islam, peace and jihad as well as Islamic perspectives on inter-community relations. I was of the firm belief that in today's context, characterised both by heightened Islamophobia as well as extremist self-styled jihadist groups that are playing no small role in contributing to Islamophobia by engaging in terrorist activities and spreading hatred for non-Muslims, it was crucial to bring to the notice of the wider, non-Urdu knowing public some of the Maulana's invaluable writings on the subject that have not as yet been rendered into English.

The introduction to the book is an edited version of a lengthy piece that I wrote on Maulana Wahiduddin Khan some years ago. In it I made a broad survey of his arguments, from within an Islamic paradigm, for peace and inter-religious dialogue. This is followed by my translations of selected essays written in Urdu by the Maulana that are contained in several of his books, in addition to some lengthy interviews that I conducted with him. These, broadly-speaking, deal with four inter-related themes – a critique of the politics and ideology of radical, self-styled Islamists who claim to be engaged in Islamic jihad; discussions about how jihad is conceived in the Quran and the authentic Hadith or traditions about the Prophet Muhammad, and how many of today's self-styled radical jihadists have deviated from this conception; Islamic teachings about the need for inter-religious and inter-community dialogue and friendship, and how many self-styled radical jihadists very obviously act against this Quranic mandate; and, finally, the need for Muslims to abandon blind following or *taqlid* of medieval jurisprudential opinions and to engage in *ijtihad* or contextual reapplication of the teachings or commandments of the Quran and Hadith with regard to various issues, including those related to war, peace, and inter-religious and inter-community relations in today's context.

Maulana Wahiduddin Khan is, undoubtedly, the most prolific writer among the contemporary Indian *ulama*. The essays that are contained in this book that I have translated from Urdu represent only a fraction of what he has written so far on issues related to Islam, peace and jihad and Islamic perspectives on inter-religious and inter-community dialogue. He has, so far, penned more than 150 books, many of which have been rendered into English and other languages. Many more of them, however, still remain accessible only in their Urdu original. *Insha Allah*, and if life permits and the Maulana allows, translating some other of his brilliant and incisive essays is the next project that I have in mind for myself.

I would like to thank the Maulana, his daughter Dr Farida Khanam, and Rajat Malhotra of the Centre for Peace and Spirituality, New Delhi, for all their help that made this work possible.

Yoginder Sikand
Bangalore
November 2009

Introduction

Maulana Wahiduddin Khan: His Life and Work

Maulana Wahiduddin Khan was born in a family of Pathan landlords in 1925 at Badharia, a village near the town of Azamgarh in the eastern United Provinces, now the State of Uttar Pradesh. His parents died when he was quite young, and he was brought up by his father's brother, Sufi Hamid Majid Khan. While his two brothers were sent to Western-style schools, the young Wahiduddin was enrolled at a *madrasa*, a traditional Islamic seminary, the Madrasat ul-Islah, in Sarai Mir, near Azamgarh, in order to train as an *alim* or Islamic scholar. There he spent six years, completing the *alim* course, and graduating in 1944.

After his graduation, Khan returned to his village instead of taking up employment in a mosque or *madrasa*, as did most of his classmates. Back with his family, he soon found himself a misfit, feeling a great chasm between himself and his brothers and other relatives, who had received a modern (that is, Western) education.

A period of great introspection followed, as Khan slowly grew disillusioned with traditional understandings of Islam that he had imbibed at the *madrasa*. He turned to agnosticism for some time, finding that his *madrasa* education had failed to provide answers to many issues facing the modern world.

The Maulana's 'rediscovery' of Islam happened in 1948, when he began reading the primary Islamic sources in their Arabic original, instead of relying on translations and commentaries in other languages. It was, in a sense, an experience akin to being 'born again', affirming a faith that was consciously chosen, rather than one inherited as part of his cultural tradition. Clearing away the cobwebs from centuries of commentary and interpretation, and approaching the Quran and the authentic Hadith directly, he came to believe, held the key to an understanding of Islam that could prove its relevance in the modern world. Khan then set about learning English on his own, reading widely the work of Western writers and philosophers. His exposure to Western literature made him realise the pressing need to present Islam in a manner that would appeal to the modern, Western-educated mind.[1]

This period of 'rediscovery' of Islam from its original sources coincided for Khan with a quest for a socially engaged spirituality. Coming under the influence of the writings of Abul Ala Maududi, founder of the Islamist Jama'at-e Islami, Khan joined the Jama'at-e Islami Hind, the Indian wing of the Jama'at, in 1949, attracted by Maududi's understanding of Islam as a comprehensive world-view and a call for radical social revolution. His commitment to the Jama'at and his skilful pen helped him move rapidly up the Jama'at's hierarchy, being appointed, in only a few years after he joined the organisation, as a member of its Central Committee, and serving as one of the senior administrators of the Jama'at's publishing house in Rampur.

Khan wrote regularly for the Jama'at's Urdu journal, and in 1955, published his first book *Naye Ahd Ke Darwaze Par* ('On the Threshold of a New Era'). This was soon followed by *Mazhab Aur Jadid Challenge* ('Islam and the Modern Challenges'), which was later translated to Arabic and became a bestseller in the Arab world, even being incorporated in the syllabus of several Arab universities. As the titles of these books suggest, Khan was particularly concerned with developing an understanding of Islam that would appeal to the modern mind while at the same time remaining firmly grounded in the original sources of Islam, which are the Quran and the authentic Hadith.

Khan, however, did not remain for long with the Jama'at. Increasingly, it suggested to him that the Jama'at's own agenda, based as it was on working towards establishing what it called an 'Islamic State' in India, was not only impractical, but also, not in keeping with what Islam expected of the Muslims of India in the situation that they found themselves in. As Khan delved deeper into Maududi's writings, he came to believe that the very basis of Maududi's understanding of Islam was faulty and mistaken, being more a reaction to Western imperialism rather than emerging from an authentic understanding of Islam itself. Faced with the challenge of European colonial rule over most of the Muslim world, Maududi Khan concluded, had developed a quintessentially political understanding of Islam, seeing the Islamic mission as based on political, and not ideological, struggle, not ruling out one's resort to violent means to attain its goals. Khan began to see this understanding of Islam as a result of 'a sense of loss,' of defeat suffered by the Muslims at the hands of the West, rather than as emanating from a deep, genuine spiritual quest.[2]

Khan also gradually came to the conclusion that the Jama'at-e Islami's political approach was ill-suited to the needs and conditions of the Muslim minority in India. Rather than mobilising themselves to work for establishing an 'Islamic State', which was not only impractical in the given situation but which would also further embitter India's Hindus, what the Indian Muslims needed to do, Khan felt, was to attempt to build bridges with people of other faiths in the country. Khan began airing his differences with the Jama'at's ideology and policies even while still a senior leader of the Jama'at, but as these differences began to grow, he decided to quit the organisation in 1962, after serving it for fifteen years.

Disillusioned with what he called the 'politically-oriented religion' of the Jama'at, Khan was attracted to what he saw as the 'God-oriented religion' preached by another Islamic revivalist movement that had its origins in India, the Tablighi Jama'at, today probably the largest Islamic movement in the world. What seems to have been most striking for Khan about the Tablighi Jama'at was its strict aloofness from party politics, focussing on individual reform rather than on attempting to establish an 'Islamic State', as the Jama'at-e Islami was doing. For a minority like the Indian Muslims, the Tablighi Jama'at—with its concern for the gradual 'Islamisation of the individual' rather than capture of the State—seemed to him to present a more sensible and pragmatic strategy, one that was in keeping with the Prophetic practice or Sunnah.[3]

Active in the Tablighi Jama'at for some years, Khan gradually became disillusioned with it, too, and by 1975 completely disassociated from it. He saw the movement's hostility to *ijtihad*, or creative application of Islamic jurisprudence to meet the challenge of changing social conditions, and what he viewed as its aversion to critical, independent and creative thinking and the rational and scientific spirit, as placing a brake on his own intellectual development, and, moreover, as a betrayal of the Islamic imperative itself.[4] Although he still remained appreciative of the role of the Tablighi Jama'at in creating Islamic awareness among ordinary Muslims, he believed that a new understanding of Islam was necessary to appeal to modern educated Indians, both the Muslims themselves as well as Hindus and others. Accordingly, in September 1976, he set up his own research institute, the Islamic Centre, based in New Delhi, launching an Urdu monthly, *al-Risala*, to propagate his own views, which he saw as presenting Islam in a modern idiom.

In its early days, the journal consisted almost entirely of articles written by Khan himself. Today, the journal has a fairly large readership both in India and overseas, and several issues of it are also available on the Internet. Besides his journal, Khan has published, to date, over two hundred books, mainly in Urdu. Some of these books have been translated into Arabic, as well as various Indian and European languages. Khan also regularly writes for various Indian newspapers on issues of contemporary importance from an Islamic perspective. Needless to say, he is one of the few Indian *ulema* to seriously engage with the largely non-Muslim 'mainstream' Indian press.

The general context for an examination of the maturation of Khan's distinct understanding of Islam and its place and role in the modern world are provided by the following: many years of close involvement in the Jama'at-e Islami and the Tablighi Jama'at; a deep concern with the growing problem of Hindu-Muslim conflict in India; the spread of Islamist movements, many of them violent, in large parts of the Muslim world; and the perceived lacunae of traditional Islamic thought. While his advocacy of a personalisation of the faith, focussing on individual reform rather than on political mobilisation, is possibly, at least partly, a result of the influence of his earlier association with the Tablighi Jama'at, his call for bold *ijtihad*, going directly to the original sources of Islam—the Quran and the Hadith—by-passing centuries of tradition and interpretation by the *ulema*, clearly distinguishes him from the Tablighis.[5] While he shares with many Islamists an insistence on the urgency of *ijtihad*, he suggests a creative interpretation of the *shariah* for very different purposes.

Khan's primary concern is to express Islam as a perfectly suitable ideology for the modern age. In his writings, he deals at great length with issues related to pluralism, inter-faith dialogue, jihad and peace, all of which he sees both the Islamists and quietists unable, if not unwilling, to seriously consider and comprehend: the Islamists, with their radical rhetoric, and the quietists such as the Tablighi Jama'at, with their refusal to look beyond formulations of traditional *fiqh* or Muslim jurisprudence.

Peace and Dialogue and the Challenge of Pluralism

Khan is among the few Indian *ulema* to have taken seriously the issue of pluralism and inter-community relations, free from the polemics and negative stereotypes that generally characterise the response of many Muslims to people of other faiths. Writing in the mid-1970s, Wilfred Cantwell Smith had remarked on the seeming inability of the Muslims of India to come to terms with a situation of being, at least in theory, equal citizens in a plural, multi-religious nation, arguing that articulating a clear Islamic position on the matter was of the greatest importance for the community.[6] This, in fact, is precisely what Khan seeks to do in many of his writings.

The predicament of the Indian Muslims, as a minority that sees itself as increasingly beleaguered, is one that Khan takes as one of his primary concerns. Khan insists that Muslims must come out of their ghettos, shed what he calls their 'persecution complex' and separatist mentality, search for opportunities that exist despite the odds that seem to weigh heavily against them, and work alongside people of other faiths in building a new society.[7] In other words, he suggests, they should be guided by pragmatic considerations rather than by misplaced idealism.[8] Muslims must not sit back in despair, Khan says, for Islam forbids despondency, branding it as a 'grave sin'. Khan quotes the Quran as saying: 'No one despairs of God's mercy except those who have no faith' (12:87).

In contrast to most Indian Muslim leaders, Khan sees the Muslim predicament as almost entirely of their own making. While recognising that Muslims in India are, indeed, largely poor and illiterate, and sometimes falling victim to organised violence, he argues that the problems that Muslims face are rooted in their having abandoned the path of Islam and straying from the teachings of their religion. Because of this, he insists, God has appointed others as an instrument to express His anger with them, punishing them for dereliction of their divine responsibilities as the *khair-e ummat* ('the best of the communities'), as the Quran describes the *ummah* of true believers. Hence, Khan argues, Muslims must not seek to blame others for their plight and, accordingly, desist from agitation or confrontation with them.[9] Since their problems are a result of God's wrath for their straying from the teachings of Islam, they must seek to win God's favour instead. If Muslims were to faithfully abide by the teachings of Islam in their own personal lives and social dealings, he argues, they would be rewarded by God. Not only would their manifold problems be resolved but they would also be granted 'victory'.[10] Hence, as Khan sees it, Muslims must turn to internal reform rather than seeking external solutions to their problems through conflict with the State or with people of other faiths. This calls for the creation of an entirely new Muslim leadership, one that seeks to lead the community to a path of construction rather than one of confrontation.

Peace and building bridges with people of others faiths, then, becomes a matter of particular urgency for Muslims, Khan argues. The growing challenge of Hindu militancy in India today has resulted in an increasing insecurity among the country's Muslims of the country. In response, some Muslim groups have called for armed conflict to defend the community in the name of jihad. Khan sees this as a dangerous development, boding ill for the interests of the community, as well as, in his view, lacking sanction in the Quran. He likens those who call for unwarranted violence against others as the false prophets referred to in the Bible and Quran, who sought to mislead the Children of Israel from the path of God, feeding them 'the wine of false pride', exaggerating their glories, provoking their emotions and promising to lead them to an imaginary paradise.[11] Instead of being motivated by worldly considerations and purely communal interests which, he says, are 'forbidden' (*haram*) in Islam and akin to the 'tribalism' (*asabiyyat*) which the Quran sternly condemns, Muslims, he writes, must act solely in accordance with the teachings of their religion.[12] Further, they must desist from seeking to promote their own worldly interests under the guise of Islam and Islamic jihad.[13]

Khan argues that Islam is synonymous with peace, enjoining upon believers the need to explore every possible avenue for peaceful negotiation of conflicts before military means can even be contemplated. He sees many such avenues open in India today, which the Muslims have failed to consider. Inter-religious dialogue assumes for him a particularly important role in this regard. He writes that the Quran encourages Muslims to engage in constructive dialogue with people of other faiths, on the basis of what they have in common—belief in the one God and the doing of righteous deeds—while emphasising that all people have the right to follow the religion of their choice. Every religion, he writes, upholds certain basic human values, such as love, compassion, peace, and concern for the poor and the marginalised, and these must form the basis of any dialogue initiative. Moreover, Islam insists that all human beings, in their capacity of being creatures of God, are brothers and sisters unto each other. Hence, he says, Islam calls upon all Muslims to live with others as 'brothers in spirit, too'. The Prophet Muhammad, he notes, is said to have exhorted Muslims to show 'respect for every human being' and 'honour one of another creed.'[14] Hence, he says, Islam calls on people of different faiths to have 'mutual respect' for each other on the basis of their common humanity while following their own religions. This, Khan believes, is the only realistic way to foster a genuine spirit of religious pluralism.[15]

Khan writes that the Muslims of India today find themselves in a position similar to that of the Prophet and his followers in Mecca, when what was then a nascent Muslim community was small and relatively powerless. Just as at this stage the Prophet concerned himself only with peaceful preaching, so, too, must the Muslims of India eschew all confrontation with others and, instead, seek to relate to them through dialogue and the peaceful propagation of Islam. What is required, then, is a contextual reading of the Quran and the Prophetic tradition, with the Meccan model providing the basic source of inspiration for today's Indian Muslims.[16] Accordingly, Khan says, Muslims must seek to build bridges with others on the basis of the values that they hold in common, and, in accordance with the Prophetic example, work along with them for the establishment of a more just, prosperous, and peaceful society. They must concern themselves with the problems and issues concerning the country as a whole, in a spirit of enlightened patriotism and love for the country, instead of thinking only of their own communal interests, such as at present,.[17] If that were to happen, Muslims, he suggests, would be able to convince others that the Islam faith can offer viable solutions to many problems affecting society at large. It is only by proving their usefulness to society as a whole that others would not only come to regard Muslims as valuable allies, but also appreciate Islam as a religion. Muslims, he exhorts, should be able to contribute their services to society and transform themselves from the status of 'takers' to that of 'givers'. Further, by removing other people's mistaken notions of Islam as a violent religion, peaceful dialogue will also help facilitate Muslims being able to join the 'mainstream of 'universal life and participate in the benefits of global economic progress.'[18] If they were to devote themselves to promoting peace in society as a whole, Khan says, they would be able to focus their energies on the economic and educational development of the community which, owing to their past 'belligerence', they have totally ignored.[19]

Efforts to promote peace must necessarily mean that Muslims should reach out to people of other faiths in a spirit of constructive dialogue. Khan is one of the few Indian *ulema* to have seriously engaged in inter-religious dialogue initiatives. He is a regular speaker and participant at meetings of various religious heads and activists. He has also wholeheartedly engaged in meetings and interactions with leaders of militantly anti-Muslim Hindu groups, such as the Rashtriya Swayamsevak Sangh (RSS). He justifies this by arguing that in India, Muslims have to learn to live alongside Hindus. Rather than looking, in vain, solely to the government to solve their problems, Muslims, he says, must seek to build better relations with all sections of the Hindus, this alone being a guarantee for the protection of their own interests. This has won him stinging critique from some Muslims, but he insists that Muslims must interact even with those who seem most vehemently opposed to them in order to impress upon them the actual teachings of Islam.

Khan's willingness to appreciate the common values that all religions hold does not, however, mean that he believes that all religions are equally valid. Khan insists that Islam is the most perfect religion, being the only one whose scripture has survived intact. 'One can safely say', he writes, 'that for a seeker after the Truth, there is [...] only one choice to make, and that is the choice of Islam, the only religion having true historical credibility'.[20] He likens the relation between Islam and other religions to that between modern chemistry and medieval alchemy: although their subject matter is the same, Islam, like modern chemistry, is based on 'facts proved by strictly scientific methods', while other religions, like alchemy, are grounded in 'unproven speculations'. This consciousness of the truth of Islam, he says, should not, however, deter Muslims from being willing to enter into dialogue with others.

This passion for dialogue is what underlies Khan's approach to issues related to peace, jihad, and inter-community relations, as emerges from the translations of some of his essays on the themes that follow in the following sections.

Endnotes

1. Interview with Wahiduddin Khan, New Delhi, 1 February, 2001.
2. Wahiduddin Khan, *Two Types of Movements* (www.alrisala.org/Articles/thought/twomvmnt.htm).
3. Wahiduddin Khan, *The Tabligh Movement*, The Islamic Centre, New Delhi, 1986.

4. Interview with Wahiduddin Khan, New Delhi, 2 February, 2001.

5. Wahiduddin Khan, *Islam Rediscovered: Discovering Islam From Its Original Sources*, Goodword Books, New Delhi, 2001, p. 70.

6. Wilfred Cantwell Smith, *Islam in Modern History*, Princeton University Press, Princeton, 1977.

7. Wahiduddin Khan, 'Factors Hindering Hindu-Muslim Unity', *The Times of India*, Mumbai, 23 March, 1993.

8. Wahiduddin Khan, *Hal Yahan Hai*, Maktaba al-Risala, New Delhi, 1985, p. 74.

9. Ibid., p.77.

10. Ibid., p. 10.

11. Ibid., p.18.

12. Ibid., p.57.

13. *Islam Rediscovered*, op. cit., p.63.

14. Wahiduddin Khan, *Islam and Peace*, Maktaba al-Risala, New Delhi, 1999, pp.43-47.

15. Wahiduddin Khan, *Islam on the Multi-Religious Society* (http://www. alrisala.org/Articles/tolerance/multirelg.htm).

16. *Islam and Peace*, op.cit., p.163. Wahiduddin Khan, *The Political Misfortunes of Muslims* (http://www.alrisala.org/Articles/india/ misfortune.htm).

17. *Hal Yahan Hai*, op.cit., p. 69.

18. *Islam and Peace*, p.194.

19. Wahiduddin Khan, *New Decision* (http://www.alrisala.org/Articles/ india/decision.htm).

20. *Islam Rediscovered*, op.cit., p.45.

1

The Concept of Jihad in Islam

The Arabic word *jihad* is derived from the root *juhd*, which means 'to strive' or 'to struggle'. It denotes the exertion of oneself to the utmost, to the limits of one's capacity, in some activity or for some purpose. This is how the word is understood in Arabic grammar. As fighting against one's enemies is also an act of exertion or striving, it is also sometimes referred to as jihad. However, the actual Arabic word for this is *qital*, not jihad. Fighting with one's enemies is something that might happen only occasionally or exceptionally. However, jihad, properly understood, is a continuous action or process that animates every day and night of the life of the true believer. Such a person does not let any hurdle affect his life, including the desire for gain, the pressure of customs, the demands of pragmatism, and the lust for wealth. All these things serve as obstacles in the path of doing good deeds. Overcoming these hurdles and yet abiding by the commandments of God is the true jihad, and this is the essential meaning of its concept. There are many references to jihad, as understood in this way, in the collections of sayings attributed to the Prophet Muhammad.

The present world is a testing ground, and its environment has been fashioned in such a way that human beings are constantly put to the test. In the course of this test, human beings are faced with numerous hurdles, to face which one must repeatedly suppress or sacrifice one's own desires or, in some cases, even one's life. Overcoming these odds and facing all sorts of difficulties and losses while remaining firm on the path of truth is the real and fundamental jihad. Those who remain steadfast on the path of this jihad will be blessed with entrance to paradise.

Jihad, in essence, is a form of peaceful action or activism. This peaceful activism can take the form of inviting others to the path of truth. The Quran advises us not to obey those who champion falsehood, and, in one verse, tells us to engage in jihad with them through the Quran. This means that one should respond to them by inviting them to the path of the truth, striving in this regard with one's utmost efforts. The jihad that this Quranic verse refers to is not physical warfare; rather, reference here is to intellectual and ideological activism. In short, it means refuting falsehood and advancing the cause of the truth with the use of peaceful means.

Qital, which is only one form of jihad, involves physical warfare. This, however, cannot be divorced from the issue of essentially peaceful jihad. If an enemy challenges one militarily or through physical force, one should still strive to the utmost possible to respond through peaceful means. Such means can be abandoned only when it is no longer possible to use them or when warfare becomes the only way to respond to the violence being unleashed. In this regard, a statement attributed to Ayesha, one of the wives of the Prophet, serves as a guiding principle. This statement is contained in the *Sahih al-Bukhari*, a book of traditions attributed to the Prophet. Ayesha reportedly remarked that whenever the Prophet was faced with two choices, he would always opt for the easier one. This means that he would prefer the easier option and ignore the more difficult one. This principle of the Prophet applies not only to routine affairs of life but also to serious matters such as war, which is itself a difficult option. A reading of the life of the Prophet reveals that he never initiated fighting on his own. Whenever his foes sought to force him into battle, he would always try to seek some means to avoid physical fighting. He engaged in fighting only when all other options have failed.

Thus, as the Prophet's practice reveals, offensive war is forbidden in Islam. Islam allows only for defensive war and that, too, only when it becomes absolutely unavoidable. In reality, in life one is always faced with the dilemma of making choices. Some options are based on peace and others on violence. The accounts of the Prophet's life indicate that in every matter he preferred the former.

A few instances from the Prophet's life are illustrative of this fact. Soon after being appointed as a prophet, he was faced with a choice between the above-mentioned two options. His mission was to end polytheism and to establish pure monotheism, belief in, and surrender to, the one God. The Ka'aba in Mecca had originally been made as a centre for the worship of the one God, but, by the time of the advent of the Prophet, some 360 idols had been installed therein. Hence, one might think that the Quran should have first instructed the Prophet to purify the Ka'aba of the idols and to remake it as a centre for monotheism. Had this been the case, it would have been tantamount to warring with the Quraish pagans of Mecca, who enjoyed leadership among the Arabs precisely because they were custodians of the Ka'aba. History tells us that at this stage the Prophet restricted himself simply to the spreading the message of monotheism instead of removing the idols from the Ka'aba. This, in a sense, is a major instance of the Prophet choosing a peaceful, as opposed to violent, option.

Choosing and abiding by the peaceful option, the Prophet carried on his preaching work in Mecca for thirteen years. Despite this, the Quraish pagans fiercely opposed him, so much so that their elders plotted to kill him. Accordingly, they armed themselves with swords and surrounded his house. This was nothing short of a declaration of war against the Prophet and his Companions. However, guided by God, the Prophet decided not to retaliate militarily, and, in the darkness of night, he left Mecca and travelled to Medina. This journey is known as the *hijrah*. The *hijrah* exemplifies the choice of the use of the peaceful option, instead of a violent one.

The 'Battle of the Trench' is another example of the Prophet's choosing the peaceful option. On this occasion, an army of the Prophet's opponents marched on to the town of Medina to attack him. This was an open declaration of war on their part. In order to avoid fighting, the Prophet arranged for a trench to be dug around the town, serving as a buffer against the attackers. Consequently, the Quraish army spent just a few days camping beyond the trench and then retreated.

The choice of a similarly peaceful option was reflected in the case of the Treaty of Hudaibiyah. The Prophet and his companions wanted to worship at Mecca, but they were stopped by the Quraish chieftains at a place called Hudaibiyah and were asked to go back to Medina. The Quraish said that they would not allow them to enter Mecca at any cost. This was, in a sense, a declaration of war. If the Prophet had proceeded with his plans of proceeding to Mecca to worship, it would have meant armed conflict with the Quraish. However, the Prophet chose not to go ahead. Instead, he peacefully accepted a one-sided treaty with the Quraish and returned to Medina. This is yet another example of the Prophet choosing the peaceful, instead of violent, option.

This practice and preference was also evident when the Prophet finally took over Mecca. On this occasion, he was accompanied by ten thousand devoted companions, who could easily have militarily defeated the Quraish of Mecca. Here, too, the Prophet did not use physical force to capture the town. Instead, he quietly travelled, along with his Companions, to Mecca and entered it. This happened so suddenly that the Quraish were unable to make any preparations against them. Consequently, Mecca was won without any bloodshed. These examples suggest that, not just in ordinary situations but also in situations of emergency, the Prophet generally resorted to peaceful, as opposed to violent, means. As indicated above, in Islam peace is the rule and war is the exception; that, too, only when it becomes unavoidable.

Keep this principle in mind and survey the world today. Today's world is very different from that of ancient times, when war was the rule and was commonly resorted to. Choosing peaceful means was very difficult. However, today the situation has completely changed. In today's world, resort to violence has become completely useless and undesirable, while the use of peaceful means alone is generally accepted. So acceptable has the peaceful option become that it has emerged as a powerful force in its own right. Today, one can press one's views peacefully, through use of the right to free expression, using modern communications, and the media. These developments have made the peaceful option even more efficacious.

As mentioned earlier, the Prophet's practice indicates that when peaceful options are available they should be used and violent means be avoided. In today's context not only are peaceful methods and options aplenty, but also, owing to various supporting factors, they are much more effective. It would not be an exaggeration to claim that in today's world, violent methods have not only become more difficult, but also, in practical terms, completely useless. In contrast, peaceful methods are easier and are also much more effective. Peaceful methods have now become the only possible and efficacious option. In this context, one can claim that violent methods have to be abandoned, or what in the language of the *shariah* is termed *mansukh* or abrogated. Now the followers of Islam have only one option to choose, and that, without any doubt, is the peaceful option, unless, of course conditions change so much that the directive, too, needs to be changed.

While it is true that in the past, violent means have occasionally been used, these were only under compulsion due to temporal factors. Now, as conditions have so changed that this compulsion no longer exists, the use of violent means is no longer necessary and is, in fact, undesirable. Under the new conditions, only peaceful methods should be used. As far as the issue of jihad is concerned, peace is the rule and war has the status of only an unavoidable exception.

According to a well-known principle in Islamic jurisprudence, certain rules can be modified in the wake of change of time and place. This means that when the context changes one must seek to re-apply the juridical rule in accordance with, and to suit, the new context. This principle applies as much to issues of war as it does to other matters. This principle thus demands that violent methods be declared as abandoned and only peaceful methods should be given the status of being sanctioned by the *shariah*.

Contemporary So-Called Jihadist Movements

Today, in various countries across the world, Muslims are involved in armed movements in the name of what they claim to be 'Islamic jihad'. However, simply by being branded as a *jihadist* movement by its leaders, no such movement can be actually considered thus. No action can be considered as a legitimate jihad unless it fully meets the conditions as laid down in Islam. Battles fought in the name of jihad without meeting such conditions cannot claim to be so. Rather, they are *fasad* or strife, the very opposite of Islamic jihad. Those who are engaged in such activities will not get the reward for jihad from God; instead, they will be considered worthy of punishment in God's eyes.

Jihad in the sense of *qital* is not a private act in the same manner as prayers and fasting. Rather, it is an act that is entirely associated with a state or government. This is clearly indicated in the Quran and the Hadith. For instance, the Quran says that in the face of intimidation by the enemy, individuals should not take any action on their own, but, instead, turn to those in charge of their affairs so that the latter can understand the matter in a proper perspective and take appropriate and necessary steps. This means that, on their own, individual members of the public cannot decide on issues of war. This is something left to governments to handle. A *hadith* report states that the Imam or leader is like a shield: war is conducted under his control and through him safety is ensured. This means that war and defence must always be left to the rulers to manage.

There is an almost unanimous opinion on this issue in the Islamic juridical tradition and almost no noted Islamic scholar has dissented from this view. The near consensus of the Islamic jurisprudents is that war can be declared only by an established government. Subjects or citizens of a State do not have the right to do so. Today, in various places, Muslims are engaged in fighting with governments in the name of jihad. Almost without exception, however, these are not really Islamic jihads. They are *fasad* or condemnable strife. None of these so-called jihads has been declared by any government. All of these self-styled jihads have been declared, and are being conducted, by non-state forces and actors. If some of these violent movements have the backing of any Muslim governments, this is being done secretly, while, according to the *shariah*, jihad on the part of a government must entail an open declaration of war. Without this, *qital* on the part of a Muslim government is illegal.

Today, the various violent movements in the name of jihad being engaged in by some Muslims are of two types: either guerrilla wars or proxy wars. Both sorts of war are completely illegal according to Islam. Guerrilla wars are unacceptable in Islam because they are led and conducted by non-state actors, not by any established government. Likewise, proxy wars are unacceptable in Islam because the governments behind them do not issue a formal and open declaration of war.

Islamic jihad, if properly understood, is a constructive and continuous process. It remains active throughout the life of a true believer. It has three aspects. Firstly, *jihad-e nafs* or the struggle against the baser self or the ego, against one's passions and wrong desires and to remain steadfast in one's commitment to lead the life that God wants for human beings. Secondly, jihad in the sense of striving, using peaceful means, to communicate God's word to all of His slaves, inspired by a compassion and concern for others, even if this is not reciprocated. This is the great jihad according to the Quran. The third form of jihad relates to confronting one's foes and to remain firmly committed to the faith under all conditions.

In the past, this form of jihad was basically a peaceful action, and so remains even today. In this sense, jihad, properly understood, is a peaceful struggle and not military or physical confrontation.

This is a translation of a chapter in Maulana Wahiduddin Khan's book, *Aman-e Alam* ('Global Peace'), Goodword Books, New Delhi, 2005, pp. 27–37.

2
Terror in the Name of Islam

Some time ago, I met a Muslim who lives in America. In the course of our conversation, he mentioned that today the image of Islam has become so negative in America that he is reluctant to admit that he is a Muslim. 'If anyone asks me my religion, I say that I follow humanism. If I tell them that I am a Muslim, they will at once brand me as a terrorist,' he bemoaned.

This man blamed the media for creating and presenting this negative image of Islam. I replied to him, saying, 'No. This image of Islam has been created by Muslims themselves. In various places, Muslims have launched violent movements ostensibly in the name of Islam, and this is what the media reports about. Because Muslims carry on these violent movements in the name of Islam, the media also attributes them and their violence to Islam itself.' Then I asked him, 'If Muslims themselves are engaged in such movements in the name of Islam, how can the media attribute these movements to anything else?'

The man replied that only relatively few Muslims were engaged in such violent or terrorist movements. Hence, he protested, it was wrong to create a negative image of Islam based on the actions of these few. My answer to him was, 'Yes, it is true that relatively few Muslims are involved in such movements, but it is also true that the vast majority of other Muslims do not openly condemn such movements. They observe a strange silence about them. Hence, and in accordance with the very principles of Islam, it would not be wrong to say that even if only a few people are directly responsible for spearheading these violent and hate-driven movements in the name of Islam, the vast majority of other Muslims are also indirectly responsible for it, too.'

This position of the Muslims is extremely worrisome. In the name of establishing 'Islamic Government' and 'The Prophetic System' and jihad, such horrendous misdeeds are being committed that are completely opposed to Islam. Far from attracting people to the religion of God, these deeds only further repel people. Those who commit such acts claim that they are engaged in setting up an Islamic or Prophetic 'System', but this is completely false. It is nothing more than a ruse to gain political power and leadership in the name of Islam. Such movements have absolutely no sanction in Islam. The aim of genuine Islamic mission is to Islamise individuals, not the government or State. Accordingly, for centuries, the Sufis focused on the Islamisation of individuals. For this they used peaceful methods and never became a source of conflict or violence. The Sufis promoted peace and humanity, while the so-called 'revolutionary Islamic' movements are producing wholly the opposite results.

One can thus safely say that the self-styled Muslim leaders of today who have spawned violent movements aimed at grabbing political power, are themselves responsible for creating the image of Islam as inseparable from hatred and violence. Through their actions, they have made Islam appear as a religion of hatred and violence, while, in actual fact, the Islam sent by God is a religion of peace and welfare for all. A true Muslim is one who is concerned about the welfare of all of humankind, not someone who is at war with humanity.

Islamic Jihad

There are certain strict conditions for a genuine Islamic jihad in the path of God. A movement that does not observe these conditions cannot be said to be an Islamic jihad. A true jihad is only that which is done in the path of God. War or conflict for the sake of power or wealth or for any other such worldly purpose cannot be considered a jihad even if those who are engaged in it claim it to be so. Rather, it is *fasad*, a source of great strife that is sternly condemned in Islam. Further, according to the Islamic *shariah*, only an established government has the prerogative to declare war or physical jihad. An individual or a group of individuals does not have this authority. No matter what complaints an individual or a group may have, they have to use only peaceful means. It is forbidden for them to resort to war or violence under any conditions.

Jihad, in the form of *qital* or physical struggle against enemies, is a wholly defensive act. Offensive *qital* is clearly forbidden in Islam. Furthermore, even if one comes under attack from another community, fighting must be sought to be avoided as far as possible. Defensive war can only be engaged in when all efforts to avoid fighting have proved unsuccessful. The opponents of the Prophet sought to engage him in war and conflict more than eighty times, but he was able to avoid fighting, except on three occasions—the battles of Badr, Uhud and Hunain—when war became unavoidable.

Taking Hostages

These days, some Muslims are resorting to violent tactics against their supposed enemies, such as hijacking and taking hostages. All such tactics are completely forbidden in Islam. Those who engage in such acts are undoubtedly bereft of the fear of God. Such terrible attacks make victims of innocent people. These deeds are cowardly and wholly against humanity as well as against the religion of God. An instance from the life of the Prophet clearly illustrates this.

Opponents of the Prophet in Mecca once captured some Muslims and kept them as prisoners. At this time, the Prophet had entered into a treaty with the Meccans at Hudaibiyah. Hence, he did not ask the Meccans to release his followers whom they had captured; the Prophet instead agreed that if any Meccans were captured by the Muslims, they would be released and sent back to Mecca. This suggests that if the opposing party captures some among one's people, it is still not permissible for us to take their people as hostages.

The Real Culprits

Who, then, are really responsible for creating a storm of hatred and violence in the name of Islam today? It is not basically those Muslim youths who are engaged in these movements. Rather, the real culprits are the so-called 'Islamic ideologues' who have misled these youths in the name of 'Islamic Revolution' which has produced such disastrous consequences. Islam's method is one of inviting others to the faith or *da'wah*, while the other, opposing method is that of politics or *siyasah*. *Da'wah* is based on peace. In contrast, politics is based on conflict and confrontation. Today's self-styled 'Islamist' ideologues have invented a political interpretation of Islam, because of which

Islamic movements have become political movements. Consequently, they have caused all those things that are worthy of blame and that are associated with politics and political movements that have come to be associated with the image of Islam.

Da'wah regards the contending party as a possible friend. In politics, it is completely the opposite: politicians regard their contenders as opponents and enemies. This is why *da'wah* generates a culture of benevolence, and politics only a culture of hate. In a society characterised by a culture of benevolence, good things will be promoted, and in a society characterised by a culture of hate, all manner of violence and strife prosper. Nothing good can ever come out of hatred.

The Real Work To Be Done

In reality, the present-day violent Muslim political movements are not just un-Islamic, but they are also completely useless. Recent history provides ample examples to exemplify this. In the first half of the twentieth century, most Muslim countries were directly or indirectly under the control of Western colonial powers. Today, all these countries are politically independent, and number more than sixty. Yet, Muslims lack any weight on the global political scene. This is because in the past, political power counted for everything, but today it has acquired a secondary status. Today, education, knowledge, science, technology and economics are more important; merely being politically independent is insufficient.

Muslim countries are today much behind others in these non-political spheres. As a result, they have little influence at the global level. Most of their people are still illiterate. In the fields of science and technology, they are still heavily dependent on the West. Most of them are economically backward. Hence, despite being nominally politically independent, they considerably lag behind others, and are dependent on them in most spheres.

Some Muslim countries claim to have undergone an 'Islamic Revolution'—for instance, Iran, Algeria, Sudan, and Afghanistan—or to be 'Islamic' States, such as Saudi Arabia and Pakistan. In fact, however, these self-proclaimed 'Islamic' States suffer the same sort of serious problems as those Muslim States that claim to be 'secular'. This is because they are as backward as the latter in the intellectual and economic fields. This is why Muslims should now focus on, and advance in, these non-political fields. Work in these fields has nothing to do with politics and political power. Such work can only be undertaken in an atmosphere of peace. For this there can be no room for hatred or violence. This is the field of constructive work, and can have nothing to do with destructive activities.

This is a translation of a chapter in Maulana Wahiduddin Khan's book, *Aman-e Alam* ('Global Peace') Goodword Books, New Delhi, 2005, pp. 103–108.

3
True Islam is Opposed to Terrorism

If properly understood, Islam is the very opposite of terrorism and has nothing to do with it. The word 'Islam' is derived from the root *s-l-m*, which means 'peace'. Hence, Islam, correctly interpreted, is a religion of peace. Naturally, a religion that describes itself as a religion of peace can have no relation with terrorism, if that religion is interpreted in the right manner. In the Quran, the Prophet Muhammad is referred to as *rahmat al-il 'alamin*, or 'mercy unto the worlds'. He is thus a source of mercy for all of humankind and not for Muslims alone. Naturally, then, his teachings, properly understood, can have no room for terrorism at all.

In a report recorded in the books of Hadith, it is said that every morning, before the *fajr* or morning prayer and after completing the *tahajjud* prayer, the Prophet Muhammad would beseech God, saying, 'Oh Allah! I bear witness that all humans are brothers of each other.' This being the case, how can there be any Islamic sanction for the killing of innocent people? All men and women are brothers and sisters unto each other. Hence, they must have love and concern for the welfare of all. This is precisely what Islam, if correctly interpreted, requires of its followers.

According to another *hadith* report, the Prophet Muhammad is said to have declared, 'All creatures are part of God's family.' This is a wonderful expression of true universalism. It clearly announces that all of humankind, irrespective of religion or community, belongs to the same family of God. In this way, this *hadith* report is a declaration of the slogan about the world being a global village which we are today so familiar with.

Given Islam's clear teaching about all creatures being members of God's family, it is ironic that some Muslims care nothing about killing innocent people, and that, too, in the name of Islam. This is truly un-Islamic. When conflicts arise between Muslims and other communities, violence is not the right approach, for it gives rise to terrorism. As the Quran instructs us, 'Reconciliation is best'. This means that the proper way to solve conflict is not through violence, which leads to terrorism, but rather, through peaceful discussion and dialogue. One must adopt constructive, not destructive, approaches to conflict resolution.

According to another *hadith* report, God gives in return for gentleness what He does not in the case of hard-heartedness. This report relates to the consequences of one's behaviour or approach. If we have a dispute or conflict with someone, fighting him or her will not solve it. The only way to resolve such conflict is through peaceful dialogue and exchange of views. This is what Islam itself demands of us.

Islam, properly understood, does not teach us to hate others. To hate others can be said to be *haram* or forbidden in Islam. Let me cite an instance in this regard. The Prophet was born in Mecca, and it was there that he announced his prophethood. Thirteen years later, he shifted to Medina. There were numerous Jews living in Medina at that time. One day, he saw a funeral procession and stood up, as a sign of respect, as it passed by. One of his followers pointed out that this was a funeral procession of a Jewish man. In other words, he indicated that the Prophet had stood up as the procession had passed despite the fact that the deceased was a Jew, not a Muslim. In reply, the Prophet responded, 'Was he not a human being?' That is to say, are not Jews also human beings? This clearly indicates that we have to respect everyone, in their capacity of being creatures of God, including Jews. This shows that terrorism has no place in Islam, if Islam is properly understood.

Terrorism can be defined as illegitimate violence resorted to in order to have one's demands met. Therefore, those who label terrorism as a jihad are making a mockery of Islam. Jihad can only be declared by a regular government or state authority, not by ordinary citizens. Today, terrorism takes, broadly, two forms: proxy war and guerilla war. I can say with full confidence that both of these forms of terrorism are *haram* or forbidden in Islam. Proxy war is illegitimate in Islam because Islam requires that a declaration of war be explicitly made before war can be actually waged, while a proxy war is, by definition, one that is unannounced and indirectly engaged in, by using local agents. Likewise, guerilla war is also forbidden in Islam because it involves civilians taking up arms against an established government in the name of jihad. It cannot be considered as a legitimate jihad because the right to declare jihad, as I mentioned earlier, rests only with the state authorities.

Let me conclude this essay by reflecting on the ongoing violence in the state of Jammu and Kashmir, which some self-styled Islamist groups claim to be a legitimate Islamic jihad. The violence that continues to rage in the State is, clearly, a combination of proxy war and guerilla war, and thus absolutely *haram* or forbidden, according to Islam. People often complain that the media is being unfair by describing this terrorism in Kashmir as 'Islamic terrorism', thereby giving Islam a bad name. But, the question is, when people who call themselves Muslim are themselves engaging in terror in the name of Islam, can we really blame the media for referring to this violence by this name? It is for Muslims to desist from this un-Islamic violence and from giving Islam a bad name by claiming terrorism to be Islamically-legitimate jihad.

This is a translation of an article by Maulana Wahiduddin Khan, titled Islam *Aur Dehshatgardi Ek Dusre Ki Zadd* ('Islam and Terrorism Are Polar Opposites'), in Farooq Argali (ed.) *Islam Aur Dehshatgardi* ('Islam and Terrorism'), Farid Book Depot, New Delhi, 2003, pp. 85–88.

4

A Critique of Religious Extremism

In the books of Hadith it is written that, once during a battle, a Muslim received a grievous injury on his head. The next morning, the man needed to have a bath, but for him to do so was dangerous, for it could make his wound ever more severe. He turned to some of his fellow Muslims and asked them what he should do. They answered that since water was available, he could not escape the rule of having a bath. He followed their instructions, but, as a result, his condition worsened and he died. When the Prophet Muhammad learned of this, he was extremely sad, and announced, 'They have killed the man. May God destroy them.'

The issue of whether or not the wounded man was obliged, according to Islamic law, to have a bath was one that involved *ijtihad* or the application of reason in interpreting the sources of Islamic law. It is evident from this story that the Prophet was greatly angered at the decision that the men had made. This indicates that making mistakes in *ijtihad* is excusable only to a certain extent. In ordinary circumstances, such mistakes might be forgiven, but in very sensitive matters, such as those that involve people's life, it is better to abstain from offering any *ijtihad*-based opinion. To do so, and, worse, to insist on one's opinion, is inexcusable. It is an indication of the loss of faith.

The above mentioned *hadith* report concerns an error of *ijtihad* that involved damage to a single individual. Naturally, an error of this sort, but on a larger scale, such as that which causes harm to a large number of people, is even more unforgivable and much more serious.

If a Mufti gives a wrong fatwa in response to a query as to whether or not one should face in the direction of the Ka'aba while bathing, there is no danger of this causing any damage to anyone's life. But a wrong fatwa about whether or not Islamic laws require a badly injured person to bathe is of a different sort, for it can seriously endanger the person's health. The two sorts of issues are not the same. In the first case, a person who makes a mistake in his *ijtihad* will be rewarded by God for his good intention in engaging in *ijtihad*, but a mistake made in the second case is an inexcusable crime. On issues on which the very fate and lives of individuals and communities crucially depend, it is incumbent on Muftis to remain silent till the very end. If, finally, they have to speak out, they should do so bearing in mind that they would have to be answerable for their opinion before God. This matter relates to the issue of violence and extremism as well.

In a *hadith* report attributed to the Prophet Muhammad, he is said to have advised his followers not to be harsh with regard to their own selves. Otherwise, he said, they would be dealt harshly with. He related that a particular community was harsh on itself and then God was also harsh with it. The remnants of that community, he said, were those who lived in churches and monasteries.

The extremism that this *hadith* report refers to is not related just to religion or to a certain form of world-renouncing and extreme monasticism. Rather, it relates to all aspects of human life. It applies to all cases where the middle path is abandoned and replaced with extremism.

The extremist lives in his own world. He knows only what he believes and wants. He is like the person who imagines that a road is empty and drives his vehicle at full-speed. Naturally, such a person can never be successful in achieving his goals. The key to success in this world is the middle path, the path of balance, which is the opposite of extremism. Extremism may be said to be an attitude or lifestyle that is contrary to God's plan of creation. Contrarily, following the balanced way or the middle-path is the means to live out one's life constructively, and in accordance with that plan. Naturally, then, extremism has no room in Islam, if Islam is properly understood.

God dislikes extremism. Those who take to the extremist path finally end up making extremism part of their very understanding of religion. The generations that follow them then feel obliged to follow precisely that path, wrongly believing it to be mandated by God. They are made to believe that if they turn their backs on extremism, they would be less committed to their religion, as they understand it, than their forebears were.

As in matters of religion, extremism with regard to other issues must also be avoided. Take, for instance, the case of the struggle for the political and economic rights of a community. For this purpose, there are, broadly, two ways of acting: one is peaceful struggle; the other is violent agitation. Peaceful struggle and activism is the best path. The violent or extremist path would only invite unnecessary suffering for the community. If it is presented as something mandated by religion, it will turn into a precedent that others will be tempted to follow, even if it does not produce the required results, because people might start believing that not adopting an extremist posture is tantamount to straying from the faith or that it is synonymous with cowardice.

Extremism, including religious extremism, indicates a profound blindness to reality and existing opportunities. It indicates that one is ruled by emotions, instead of by reason. It indicates haste and impulsiveness, instead of far-sightedness and gradualism. It reflects a total disregard for one's own or one's community's limits. It is analogous to a man who takes burning coals in his hand in order to gauge their heat, or who uses his head as a hammer in order to break a boulder. Action of this sort clearly trespasses the set limits, and those who take to this path can never succeed in this world.

This is a translation of a section in Maulana Wahiduddin Khan's book, *Islam Aur Intiha Pasandi* ('Islam and Extremism') Positive Thinkers Forum, Bangalore, n.d., pp. 54–58.

5

Extremism and the Misinterpretation of Islam

The Quran says that Cain, son of the first man, Adam, killed his own brother, Abel, due to some personal reason. After that, the Quran declares:

On that account: We ordained for the Children of Israel that if anyone slew a person—unless it be for murder or for spreading mischief in the land—it would be as if he slew the whole people: and if anyone saved a life it would be as if he saved the life of the whole people. Then although there came to them Our Messengers with Clear Signs, yet even after that, many of them continued to commit excesses in the land (Surah Al-Maidah: 32).

This suggests that killing innocents is completely forbidden according to God's law and that it is a heinous crime. However, human beings have always acted against and disobeyed this law. They have resorted to killing others for what they see as their own interests or out of revenge or, as now, on an increasingly menacing scale, out of ideological reasons. I wish to discuss this latter form of violence, or what can be called 'ideologically-driven killing'. By this I mean killing of innocent people for which ideological justification is sought. This sort of violence completely overlooks the distinction between innocents and others and leads to indiscriminate killings. But, because ideological justification is sought to be provided for these killings, it does not prick the conscience of those who engage in such violence. Their ideology leads these people to believe that the violence that they perpetrate is for the cause of Truth.

A horrific instance of this sort of 'ideological violence' was that perpetrated by some Communists in the early twentieth century. According to their understanding of the theory of dialectical materialism, the revolution that they sought could only come about through killing 'class enemies'. This led to the massacre of literally millions of people in different parts of the world.

A second, even more frightening form of 'ideological violence' was that which emerged in parts of the Muslim world in the first half of the twentieth century. Two Muslim parties were particularly responsible for developing and spreading this ideology: the Ikhwan ul-Muslimin in the Arab world and the Jama'at-e Islami in South Asia. The Ikhwan's slogan was 'The Quran is our Constitution, and armed jihad is our Path, and through this we will establish Islam throughout the world.' From Palestine to Afghanistan, and from Chechnya to Bosnia, wherever violence was resorted to in the name of 'Islamic Jihad', it was all a product of this ideology.

Likewise, the Jama'at-e Islami developed the theory that all the systems prevailing in the world today are 'evil' or *taghuti*. It claimed that it was the duty of all Muslims to struggle to destroy these systems and establish the 'Islamic system' in their place. It claimed that this work was so necessary that if by warning or admonition this did not happen, the followers of Islam should resort to violence to snatch the keys of power from the upholders of 'evil' and establish 'Islamic Governments' across the whole world. The violence that is happening today in Pakistan and Kashmir in the name of Islam is entirely a result of this fabricated ideology.

Before and after 9/11, the horrific violence that happened and is still happening in the name of Islam could be said to be directly or indirectly a result of these two self-proclaimed 'revolutionary' movements. The origin of the deviant ideology of the founders of these movements lies in their being unable to understand the difference between a group or party (jama'at) and the State. They considered what is actually the responsibility of an established State or government to be the duty of the jama'at or group that they had founded. According to Islam, the declaration and conduct of jihad, in the sense of qital or physical warfare, and the establishment of Islamic laws related to collective affairs is solely the responsibility of the State. It is completely forbidden in Islam for non-State actors to form parties in order to engage in struggles or movements for this purpose.

The limits or scope of a jama'at in Islam are illustrated in the following Quranic verse:

Let there arise out of you a band of people inviting to all that is good, enjoining what is right, and forbidding what is wrong: they are the ones to attain felicity (Surah Al-e Imran: 104).

In this verse of the Quran, the word 'band of people' refers to a group and not to a political party. My reading of the above-quoted

Quranic verse leads me to believe that non-State actors can establish a *jamaʿat* only for two purposes: Firstly, for peaceful invitation to the good; and secondly, using peaceful means, for guiding and correcting people. The former refers to conveying the message of Islam to non-Muslims, and by 'enjoining what is right, and forbidding what is wrong' is meant the fulfillment of the duty of advising Muslims to take the right path. Other than this, forming *jamaʿat*s for political agitation is forbidden. It is an impermissible and condemnable innovation which has no sanction in Islam.

The ideological perspective that the founders of the Ikhwan ul-Muslimin and the Jamaʿat-e Islami created themselves was against the *shariah* as well as against nature. Unnatural ideologies such as this inevitably begin with violence and end in hypocrisy. As long as people are hypnotised by their own romantic ideas, they remain so zealous in the cause of their supposed 'Revolution' that they can even consider suicide-bombing as legitimate, wrongly giving it the name of martyrdom. But, when the hard rock of reality forces their zeal to cool off, they resort to sheer hypocrisy: that is, at the intellectual level they continue to cling to their ideology, but in practical terms, they fully adjust to reality in order to protect their own worldly interests.

This is a translation of a chapter in Maulana Wahiduddin Khan's book, *Aman-e Alam* ('Global Peace'), Goodword Books, New Delhi, 2005, pp. 95–97.

6
Peace in a Plural Society

I ndia won its political independence from the British in 1947, but
it was accompanied by the tragic Partition of the country. The
Partition was based on the 'two-nation' theory. Far from solving
the problem of communal conflict between Hindus and Muslims,
however, it only further exacerbated it. Prior to the Partition, the
conflict was between two communities; with the Partition, it now
became one between two countries.

The Partition was accompanied by horrific communal violence
on both sides of the newly created border. It has since continued
unabated. In order to address the issue, the first Indian Prime Minister,
Jawaharlal Nehru, called a national level conference in October 1961.
At the conference it was decided to set up a National Integration
Council to deal with matters related to communal harmony. The
second conference of the Council was held in June 1962. Many
speakers orated on the occasion, suggesting various measures to

promote communal harmony. Yet no action was taken on their suggestions. The third meeting of the Council was called by the then Prime Minister Indira Gandhi in Srinagar in 1968, where legal action was suggested against those spreading communal conflict. Some other steps were also mooted. Still, nothing practical came out of this, and even today, the situation in the country is about the same as it was in 1947 as far as the issue of communalism is concerned.

What is the reason for this failure? My answer is that, to a large extent, this is because the issue has been seen simply one to do with the question of law and order. However, in actual fact, the nature of the matter is something quite different. It is actually deeply related to the lack of intellectual and social awareness. Thus, the problem of communalism requires a change in people's way of thinking and sense of discernment.

Religious Differences

I wish to clarify some basic issues which relate to this vital question of properly educating people about the issue of communalism. The first has to do with the issue of religious differences. There are, in fact, obvious differences between the various religions. For instance, some religions believe in monism, others in monotheism, yet others in polytheism, and some believe that there are 330 million gods, or even more. Some religions preach the discovery of truth by oneself, while others believe that such truth is revealed by God through messengers.

Some people think that these religious differences are themselves the major cause for communal conflict. They claim that communal conflict can be stopped only when these differences are put an end to. 'Bulldoze them all,' say some extremists. This, of course, is completely impractical.

In the face of the reality of religious differences, some other people seek to argue that all religions are, actually, one and the same. But this is like extracting portions from the Constitutions of different countries and putting them together in a single book and then claiming that all the Constitutions of the world are the same. Naturally, this will not be acceptable to the citizens of the different countries, who will outright reject such a claim since it is false.

I have often pondered on the question of religious differences, and, on the basis of my study of different religions, believe that to say that all religions are the same is not true. In actual fact, religions differ from each other in numerous ways. Hence, to claim that the teachings of all the religions are identical is quite fallacious. Even if, by some unknown means, it could be argued that the texts of the different religions are, in actual fact, basically the same, there are multiple and conflicting interpretations of each of these texts, as a result of which each religion is further divided into numerous sects.

Such variations are not limited to religion alone. The entire world is based on, and characterised by, differences. These differences are so pervasive that no two things or people in the world are wholly identical. As someone has very rightly said, 'Nature abhors uniformity'. When difference is itself a law of nature, how can religion be an exception to this rule? Just as there is diversity in everything else in the world, so too is there variety in religion. We have not thought it necessary to do away with differences in other matters, but, instead, have agreed to disagree. We should adopt this same practical approach in matters of religion. Here, too, we should accept diversity and differences and seek to promote unity despite the diversity, instead of hankering after an imaginary unity by trying to do away with this diversity. The only way to solve the issue of religious differences is to follow one and respect all.

Cultural Differences

The issue of cultural differences is also a vexing one. Distinct social groups are characterised by cultural differences. Some people regard these differences as the root of communal conflict. They argue that to end this conflict, these differences should be wiped off, and a single, common culture should be imposed on everyone so that what they call 'cultural unity' can thereby be promoted. Likewise, some people seek to overcome cultural or religious differences by advocating what they call 'social re-engineering' or 'cultural nationalism'. These are completely impractical approaches. They are tantamount to 'cultural bulldozing'. Culture cannot be made or destroyed by individuals at will in this manner. It cannot be formulated and prepared by someone sitting in a drawing-room. Rather, it is a product of a long process of historical development.

In the wake of the Second World War, numerous ideologues in different parts of the world began calling for the establishment of a mono-cultural society in the name of promoting national unity. This mono-cultural approach was tried, for instance, in Canada, but it proved completely impractical and soon had to be abandoned. Canada has since officially adopted multiculturalism as its policy and has abandoned mono-culturalism for good. This happened in the United States as well. After the Second World War, a movement to promote what was called 'Americanisation' emerged, which sought to impose a single culture on all Americans. This also failed, and now in America, multiculturalism is the recognised official policy.

Cultural differences are not merely a matter of variations between two communities. Such differences are to be found among different sub-groups in each community. It is impractical, indeed impossible, to do away with these differences. Cultural and religious homogeneity are not in accordance with the principles of nature and of history. This has never happened in the past, nor can it happen in the future, for culture follows its own logic of evolution and cannot be formulated by someone and then imposed on all others. Therefore, the only practical way to come to terms with differences between communities—whether religious or cultural—is to adopt the approach of 'Live and Let Live' and of peaceful tolerance and co-existence. Engaging in conflict in order to seek to do away with these differences will be of no avail. Far from eliminating differences, it will only magnify them, making the problem even more intractable.

Some people claim that India belongs to the Hindus, and that they are devoted to this country. They claim that this is not the case with the Muslims of India, whose centres of devotion—Mecca and Medina—are located outside India. That is why, they allege, Muslims cannot be loyal to India. I differ with such arguments. If a Hindu is devoted to the temple of Somnath, in Gujarat, this does not mean that he is not devoted to a temple elsewhere. If someone loves his mother, it surely does not mean that he has no love for his father. Similarly, if an Indian Muslim has an emotional bonding with Mecca and Medina, it does not mean that he has no love for India. Surely, human beings, whether Hindus, Muslims or others, are expansive enough to contain within them multiple loves and bondings. This is something that every man and woman personally knows and experiences. As a Western philosopher very aptly put it, 'I am large enough to contain all these contradictions.'

Religion and Politics

Very often, religion is dragged into communal controversies and repeatedly, political and communal controversies are turned into religious issues. This further ignites peoples' passions and exacerbates communal conflicts. As a result, many people have turned against religion itself. They say that human beings do not need religion, and that religion must be destroyed and only then is communal harmony possible.

I think this is an extremist response to an extremist issue, a secular extremist response to religious extremism. This is not a desirable approach. I believe that, in itself, religion is not a problem. What is a problem is the political exploitation of religion by some people and forces. Hence, it is this—the exploitation of religion, rather than religion itself—that needs to be combated and ended.

Religion has two parts: the personal and the collective. The former refers to beliefs, worship, morality, and spiritualism. The latter pertains to political and social laws. I believe that the right approach would, in general conditions, be to focus only on the former. All effort should be placed on promoting the true spirit of religion. As for the political and social laws of religion, they should not be highlighted until such time as society is itself prepared for them, because they can be established only if the entire society collectively is willing to abide by them. Only when that happens should the question of this aspect of religion be raised. This can be called a practical division between religion and politics. That is, while in terms of theory or principle, politics can continue to be considered part of religion, in the face of practical realities, the enforcement of the political rules of religion can be postponed. This is a wise and practical approach. In this way, the demands both of religion and of politics will be respected: that of religion in the present, and of politics, in the future. On the other hand, if this pragmatic policy is not adopted and both aspects of religion are sought to be focussed on, the demands of neither religion nor politics can be respected.

Religious Beliefs and Communal Harmony

Muslims have some complaints about certain Hindu beliefs, which they think hamper communal harmony. I will not discuss this matter here, but I will only advise Muslims that they should abide by the Islamic principle of tolerance. On the other hand, Hindus have some complaints against, or misunderstandings about, Muslims, and these I would like to dwell upon now. In particular, I would like to discuss some Islamic terms which are, or can become, causes of misunderstanding between Hindus and Muslims.

Before that, I want to make a brief diversion. It has become common practice that if a Muslim does something wrong, Hindus write and speak against him. And vice versa. From the point of view of social reform, this approach is absolutely wrong. The opposite should happen instead. If a Muslim does wrong, Muslim *ulema* and scholars must speak against him; and if a Hindu does wrong, Hindu leaders must do likewise. It is like if a child does something wrong, his own father is the first to scold him. The father does not wait for the neighbours to come and admonish him. In any case, if he is scolded by his neighbours instead of his father, it will have no meaningful effect on him. This is because, quite naturally, one listens more to the admonishments of one's close relations and, accordingly, seeks to reform one's self. If someone who is not one's own does the scolding or admonition, one takes it in a different spirit, as a challenge to one's pride. This has no positive impact. This principle must be carefully borne in mind when it comes to the question of promoting communal harmony.

Community, Nation, and Nationalism

Let me come back to the discussion of some Islamic terms that need explanation. Clarifying their real meaning can help in promoting better relations between Muslims and people of other faiths. On the other hand, incorrect interpretation of these terms can only further magnify differences between them.

The first term is *qaumiyat* or 'nationality' or 'community'. From the Quran it appears that the prophets addressed their people, including those who did not follow the true faith, as people who belonged to their own community (*qaum*). Hence, the believers and non-believers shared the same community or nationality. In other words, nationality is determined by one's homeland, not by one's religion. The Arabic word to denote the community formed by adherence to a common religion is not *qaum*, but *millat*. In today's world, one's homeland, not one's religion, determines one's nationality, and Islam agrees with this principle.

In this regard, the 'two-nation' theory—the claim that the Hindus and Muslims of India are two separate *qaum*s or nations—is undoubtedly wholly un-Islamic. According to this theory, articulated by the proponents of a separate Muslim State of Pakistan before 1947, the Muslims of India were a separate nation and all other Indians belonged to another nation. This argument was wrong even from the Islamic point of view. The true Islamic position is that the Muslims of India should regard themselves as belonging to the same nationality as other Indians, just as all the prophets of

God regarded even people who did not accept God's faith but who belonged to their communities as members of the same nationality or community.

Some people take an extremist position in defining the concept of nationality, so much so that they equate it with religion. This is a case of ideological extremism. Some modern Islamic scholars have interpreted Islam in such an extremist manner that they have branded all other systems other than Islam as evil and false. They declared it illegal for Muslims to live under any such system, so much so that they even argue that under such systems no Muslims should receive government education, seek government employment, vote in elections or approach the country's courts to have their disputes solved. They claim that all this is *haram* or forbidden in Islam.

This notion of so-called wholly evil and false systems is the product of some extremist minds, and does not have anything to do with the Islam of God and the Prophet. This is why practical realities have forced many of those who once upheld this erroneous notion to abandon it. The same happened in relation to the issue of nationality. Some extremists had gone to the extent of presenting nationalism as a complete religion by itself. This ideology was also, over time, exposed as hollow in the face of empirical reality. Consequently, in general, today nationalism is understood in roughly the same natural manner in which it is portrayed in the Quran.

Most Indian Muslim leaders of the first half of the twentieth century could not properly appreciate or understand these issues. They adopted an unnatural and extremist stance with regard to nationalism, declared the concept of nationalism as determined by one's homeland, instead of religion, to be un-Islamic, and claimed that this sort of nationalism threatened to take the status enjoyed by religion. This, of course, went against the actual Islamic notion of nation. Strangely, most *ulema* and Muslim intellectuals of that period considered this political issue to be a matter of life and death for Islam as a religion, while, in actual fact, no political upheavals can ever pose a challenge to the eternal truth of Islam. Some Indian Muslim scholars of that tome even declared that the collapse of the Ottoman Caliphate was tantamount to the decline of the Islamic *shariah*! This has never happened nor can it ever happen. The period of the four 'Righteously-Guided' Caliphs came to an end but Islam continued to spread. And it continued to expand even after the Umayyad and Abbasid Empires collapsed, and also after Muslim rule in Spain and that of the Fatimids in Egypt and the Mughals in India came to an end. The decline of these Muslim Sultanates could not and did not cause any decline of Islam.

Kufr and Kafirs

Some people claim that the notions of *kufr* and *kafir* are a major stumbling block to communal harmony. However, this is a misunderstanding which has nothing to do with the Quran as properly understood. The word *kufr* literally means to 'deny', and the word *kafir* means 'one who denies'. *Kufr* can be an attribute of an individual; it is not the ethic name for a group. The investigation of *kufr* with regard to any person can happen when he has been invited to the faith in the manner that the prophets engaged in, and this is carried on till its end by presenting proper and requisite proofs, or what is called *etemam al-hujjat*. Without this sort of invitation it is not proper to declare that a particular person has engaged in *kufr* or 'denial'. Likewise, it is not right for ordinary people to specifically claim a person or a group to have become *kafir*. The act of *kufr* is actually related to one's intentions, and God alone knows what these are. That is why it is only for God and His Prophet, who has been given knowledge by God, to openly and clearly declare and specify if and when a particular person is a *kafir* or 'denier'.

The Term *Dar ul-Harb* or 'Abode of War'

The term *dar ul-harb* or 'abode of war' came into being after the death of the Prophet, probably in the period of Abbasid rule. The term is not found in the Quran or the Hadith. This clearly shows that the term was coined by jurists based on their own reasoning (*ijtihad*), and is not mentioned or used in the original Islamic scriptures. And, that which is *ijtihadi*, a product of human reasoning and reflection, can be right or wrong. In my opinion, the term and concept of *dar ul-harb* reflects an *ijtihadi* error. The Prophet faced difficult challenges but he never declared any area as *dar ul-harb*. I feel that the Quran and Hadith both indicate a different sort of notion of 'abode': what can be called the *dar ul-da'wah* or 'abode of invitation to the faith'. This is what is in accordance with the Islamic spirit. Islam regards all people as those who should be invited to or addressed by its message, irrespective of whether these people are at peace or at war with its followers.

The Notion of Jihad

Due to the erroneous interpretations of some Muslims, the notion has been created that jihad means physical warfare. These Muslims believe that they are God's representatives on earth, and that they are charged with the responsibility of establishing God's government here and forcing people to obey God's laws. This understanding of jihad is undoubtedly wrong and has nothing to do with the correct understanding of the Quran and the Prophet's practice.

The notion that reforms can be brought about through force, especially in a plural society, is unacceptable. In plural societies, no community can seek a right for itself which it is not willing to allow to others. If a community thinks that it has the right to engage in war ostensibly for the sake of God or for social reform, it will have to concede the same right to other communities, too. What will then happen is that in the name of reform, all the communities will be at war with each other. And then, instead of any reform, a never-ending spiral of conflict and violence will ensue. In fact, there can be only one acceptable form of violence, and that is violence in self-defence. Other than this, there is no sanction for any sort of war.

Related to this is the memory of violent misdeeds of the past, in the age of monarchy. At that time, it was thought that the king was superior to the law and that he could do whatever he wanted. Accordingly, almost all kings engaged in such deeds that had no legal or moral sanction. Some Muslim rulers of India, too, did the same. For instance, Mahmud Ghaznavi destroyed the Somnath temple and looted its treasury. Likewise, it is said that Aurangzeb destroyed a temple in Benaras and built a mosque in its place. The examples go on.

Such deeds were committed by kings all over the world in those days. All that is now part of ancient history. While in many countries this has been forgotten, it is not the case in India, where it has become the cause of considerable bitterness between Hindus and Muslims, leading to communal conflict and posing a major challenge in the path of promoting communal harmony.

The basic reason for this, I believe, is that Muslim *ulema* and scholars have wrongly depicted the Muslim kings of India as 'Islamic' rulers, and consider them to be a part of the history of Islam as a religion. In fact, however, the status of these rulers was merely that of kings who belonged to certain dynasties. It is completely wrong to consider their rule as 'Islamic' rule. These two things are totally different. But because this difference was not kept in mind, the events that were associated with particular Muslim kings or Muslim dynasties came to be associated in people's minds with Islam as a religion. Many Muslims made the mistake of imagining the period of Muslim kings as a source of Islamic pride and as part of the history of Islam as a religion, considering it as a proof or expression of the supremacy of Islam. On the other hand, many Hindus started demanding what they called the addressing or reversal of historical wrongs. Naturally, both these stances have only resulted in further conflict.

Both sides are at fault, I believe. The fault of many Muslims is that they are not ready to re-look the history of these Muslim rulers because they wrongly believe this to be part of their religious history. The fault of many Hindus is that they are not willing to forget the past. They insist on what they say is the righting of historical wrongs, even if this makes for even more conflict in the present. Both sides need to be pragmatic. Muslims should not treat the Muslim rulers of the past as 'Islamic rulers', but, instead, look upon their reign as simply that of certain dynasties. They should disown the un-Islamic and immoral deeds that many of these rulers committed. They should openly condemn them for this, including Mahmud Ghaznavi or Aurangzeb, or anyone else. At the same time, Hindus should seek to forget the past because, as the saying goes, 'The past is past'. They should desist from emotionalism in this regard and adopt a pragmatic and realistic approach. Hindus should remember that historical wrongs have always happened but still no one has been able to remedy any of them. To seek to right historical wrongs is foolish, and can only destroy the present and the future while not being able to change what has already happened. This is completely against the law of nature.

Unfortunately, however, this trend of thinking is deeply-rooted in India. On the other hand, those countries that have sought to forget their past and concentrate, instead, on building their present have achieved major successes. One example is Japan. In the aftermath of the Second World War, Japan did not seek to correct the wrongs committed against it by America, but, instead, focussed on trying to rebuild itself. The result: Japan is today an economic superpower. In contrast, India tried to rectify historical wrongs, and that only further exacerbated the country's backwardness.

To come back to where I started, let me repeat that tolerance and acceptance of differences alone can ensure peace in a plural society. It is a law or principle of nature that there should be such differences between various social groups. That is why communal harmony cannot come about by seeking to destroy these differences. Rather, this can be possible only by accepting them. To seek to put an end to these differences is to seek to defy a basic natural law, and, obviously, this cannot succeed. No group or individual can defy and defeat natural laws. That is why pragmatism demands that, as far as the issue of religious and cultural differences is concerned, we must abide by the principle of acceptance rather than resort to conflict. Accept differences in order to create unity, because it is impossible to seek to establish unity by suppressing differences.

This is a translation of a chapter in Maulana Wahiduddin Khan's book, *Aman-e Alam* ('Global Peace'), Goodword Books, New Delhi, 2005, pp. 142–160.

7

On the Terms *Kafir* and *Kufr*

According to Marxism, as it is generally interpreted, human society is divided into two basic classes: the working class and the bourgeoisie. The word *bourgeoisie* is of French origin. In the beginning it denoted the middle classes, but later, when it was employed as a key term in Marxist discourse, it came to be understood in a derogatory sense. Consequently, in Marxist analysis, the bourgeoisie came to be regarded as the source of all social ills, while the working class was considered to be the epitome of virtue.

Somewhat the same thing has happened with the term *kafir*. In the beginning, the term simply meant what its dictionary meaning denotes: 'one who denies'. Eventually, however, it came to be used in a derogatory sense, and today this latter sense in which the term is generally understood is the source of much conflict between Muslims and others.

ON THE TERMS *KAFIR* AND *KUFR* ♦ 43

Let me refer to an instance to illustrate the possible consequences of the wrong use of the term *kafir*. The noted poet Muhammad Iqbal penned a Persian couplet in which he mentioned his Hindu Pandit origins, referring to himself as a *Brahman zada* or 'descendant of a Brahmin'. Now, the term *Brahman zada* is not seen as offensive by anyone. Suppose, however, it is replaced by the term *kafir zada* or 'descendant of a *kafir*'. Lovers of Iqbal's poetry would surely react in horror. This is because the term *kafir* has come to be widely perceived and used in a derogatory sense.

The general usage of the terms *kafir* and *momin* ('believers') by Muslims causes a great deal of anguish for many non-Muslims. So much so that some extremists opposed to Muslims and Islam have even demanded that the word *kafir* be expunged from the Islamic lexicon, claiming that till this is done Muslims and non-Muslims can never live in amity with each other.

In fact, the misuse of the word *kafir* is not something that only extremists in other communities are vehemently opposed to. To be honest, it has become a major problem for many Muslims themselves. In today's age, Muslims and non-Muslims live and work together, and, in this context, many educated Muslims feel that they cannot properly adjust to a pluralistic situation while continuing to uphold traditional understandings of the term *kafir*. Consciously or otherwise, many of them feel that several aspects of the sort of Islam that they have been reared on have lost their relevance in today's age. They have no idea how they can live respectably in society today if they continue to cling to this sort of Islam. I know of a certain very well-educated Muslim man who lives in Delhi, and who often meets me. He says that although he was born in a Muslim family he has lost faith in Islam. Democracy, he tells me, is his religion, not Islam, because, according to him, Islam sharply divides humankind into *momin*s and *kafir*s, while democracy regards all human beings as equal.

So, as I just mentioned, this issue has become a very real and serious one for many Muslims today. It is imperative, therefore, to seriously address it. This is essential in order to answer the questions people are today asking about the contemporary relevance of Islam, as well as to help create a climate wherein Muslims and people of other faiths can live together amicably.

If the issue is studied carefully and deeply, it emerges that the entire question is based on gross misunderstanding. In the general Muslim understanding, the term *kafir* is seen as synonymous with non-Muslim. Consequently, most Muslims think that anyone who is not a Muslim is a *kafir*. However, this is a completely wrong notion. The word *kafir* is not synonymous with non-Muslim.

According to the *shariah*, the role of true Muslims is that of *da'i*s or those who invite others to the path of God. The status of non-Muslims, therefore, is that of *mad'u*, or those who are to be invited to God's path. This relationship between *da'i* and *mad'u*, between true Muslims and others, necessarily demands that true Muslims, as *da'i*s, must constantly seek to maintain good and friendly relations with people of other faiths. It is said that a shopkeeper must always be customer-friendly. Likewise, a true Muslim must always be *mad'u*-friendly.

A true *da'i* must be inspired by a genuine sense of concern, love and welfare for the *mad'u*. If that is really the case, the *da'i* would never tolerate using any term that might stir hatred in the heart of the *mad'u*. In addition, a true *da'i* can never have hatred in his heart for the *mad'u*.

The ancient Aryan invaders of India contemptuously referred to the indigenous people of the country as *mleccha*s. Likewise, medieval

Christian scholars referred to Muslims as 'infidels'. Both terms were used in a derogatory sense, and those whom these terms were used to refer to obviously did not approve of them. The proper way in such cases is to use terms that do not have such derogatory notions. Unfortunately, Muslim scholars have not adopted a proper approach in this regard. In their writings and their translations of the Quran, they have indiscriminately used the term *kafir* to mean 'infidels'. In the Indian context, this has led to much misunderstanding and conflict between Hindus and Muslims. And because the term *kafir* has been used by the *ulema* in this sense, it has created a particular sort of mindset among Muslims generally, as is reflected in the writings and speeches of many Muslim scholars. It has played a major role in fashioning an entirely negative approach in the Muslim community in general towards people of other faiths. It has built up a pronounced sense of 'Muslims versus Others', 'We versus Them', which is very unfortunate and lamentable.

My own reading of the Quran leads me to believe that when it says, 'Say, "You who deny the Truth [...]"' (109:1), using the term *kafirun* for this, it refers only to the Quraish pagans of Mecca of the Prophet's time who, despite the Prophet having provided them all the proofs of his divine mission, rejected and opposed him. It was then that God declared that they had become *kafir*s or deniers of the truth in His eyes. Nowhere else in the Quran has any other group been declared in such clear and specific terms as *kafir*. This way of addressing people does not, I believe, apply to other non-Muslims, who should be addressed as human beings, rather than as *kafir*s.

More on the Term *Kafir*

As I indicated earlier, the Arabic word *kufr* means 'denial', and the related term *kafir* denotes 'one who denies', that is 'one who refuses to accept'. Thus, the word *kafir* denotes an individual character rather than being a label for a specific community or race. In many English translations of the Quran, the word has been translated as 'unbelievers', but this, I feel, is wrong. An unbeliever is someone who does not believe, but a *kafir* is a person who refuses to believe despite all the proofs of God having been presented to him in an appropriate way.

In the early part of the Prophet's mission, as evident in the initial verses of the Quran, the people he addressed were not referred to as *kafir*s, but, rather, as people. For instance, addressing the Prophet the Quran says, 'O Messenger, deliver whatever has been sent down to you by your Lord. If you do not do so, you will not have conveyed His message. God will defend you from mankind (*al-nas*). For God does not guide those who deny truth' (5:67). In this verse, God says that He would protect the Prophet from 'mankind' (*al-nas*), and does not use the word *al-kuffar* or *kafirun* or *kafir*s. There are numerous such verses in the Quran that indicate the use of the general word *insan* ('people') or related words to refer to all human communities, irrespective of religion.

It was only after thirteen years of the Prophet's struggling to present the Quraish of Mecca of his time all the required proofs of his mission while addressing them as 'people' that, after they deliberately denied him, the above-mentioned Quranic commandment 'Say, "You who deny the Truth [...]"' (109:1) was revealed. And, that, too, was an announcement from God Himself. It was not the Prophet's own statement.

The Difference Between Deeds and the Doer

Elsewhere in the Quran, the words *kufr* and *kafir* have been employed in the sense of referring to certain deeds or acts that are tantamount to *kufr*, and the person who does this is a *kafir* in God's eyes. However, other than with regard to the Quraish pagans of Mecca, and that too only after the Prophet's mission among them for thirteen long years which they rejected, there is no specific declaration in the Quran labeling any particular community as *kafir*. From this it appears that while a *da'i* or an Islamic scholar can point out that a particular deed amounts to *kufr*, he does not have the right to declare any particular community as *kafirs*. As I mentioned above, the word *kafir* relates to a certain set of actions, and is not the name of or label for any community.

This point can be further clarified with the help of a *hadith* report attributed to the Prophet which talks about the sin of a Muslim deliberately abandoning his regular prayers and linking this with *kufr*. In this context, it is acceptable for someone to appeal to Muslims in general to regularly pray and also to tell them about the grave implications of abandoning regular worship. But, it would be totally incorrect if he were to prepare a list of Muslims in his area who do not regularly worship and then specifically name them as having become *kafirs* because of this sin.

In exactly the same way, a true Muslim who calls people to the path of God can, on the basis of Quranic teachings, point out the actions which lead people to be seen as *kafirs* in the eyes of God. But he would be exceeding his boundaries if he were to address non-Muslim individuals and communities by name and declare that so-and-so non-Muslims are *kafirs*.

Hence, on the matter of *kufr* and *kafir* it is crucial to make a distinction between an act or deed of *kufr* and the person who commits that act or deed. It is only God's prerogative to make a specific declaration in this regard, and that He has done just once, with regard to the Quraish deniers and opponents of the Prophet in Mecca to whom the Prophet had provided complete proofs of God's revelation. With regard to the rest of humanity, God will decide Himself, and this would be made known in the Hereafter. Hence, the task of a true Muslim is simply to invite others to the path of God, not to declare people to be *kafirs*.

Consequently, in my opinion, from the Islamic point of view the status of non-Muslim communities all over the world, including that of the Hindus of India, is simply that of human beings (*insan*). None of these communities can be branded as *kafirs*, because as of yet the essential conditions that characterised thirteen years of the Prophet's preaching in Mecca among the Quraish, only after which the Quraish were declared as *kafirs*, have not been fulfilled. Likewise, it is incorrect to term them as 'deniers' (*munkir*).

I believe that the roots of many of the conflicts that characterise relations between Muslims and non-Muslims are essentially communal and economic. These are basically conflicts about worldly or material interests, and cannot be considered to be religious as such. Muslims must take the initiative to desist from these conflicts over worldly or material interests, and focus all their intention on their real mission, which is to invite people to the path of surrender to God.

Investigating *Kufr*

When can it be established with regard to a particular person that he has become a 'denier' (*munkir*)? The Quran provides an answer to this. The revelation of the Quran started in 610 C.E. in Mecca, and, through the Quran, the Prophet invited the Meccans to the path of worship of the one God. In this period, he never referred to his fellow Meccans as *kafirs*. Instead, he referred to them as 'human beings' or by similar terms, such as 'Quraish' or 'my community'. He conveyed to them God's message while considering them part of his own community (*qaum*). This, therefore, shows that the words *kafir* and *kufr* relate to a particular attribute and not to an entire community as such.

In his mission to invite the people of Mecca to God's path, the Prophet was filled with a sense of deep concern for the welfare of those he was addressing, and even though they heaped all sorts of oppression on him he always beseeched God to guide them. The Prophet continued to do this steadfastly throughout the thirteen long years after receiving his prophethood in Mecca. Even after that, he did not refer to these people as *kafirs* on his own. It was only later that God revealed this commandment 'Say, "You who deny the Truth [...]"' (Quran 109:1). From this it appears that only after these thirteen years of the Prophet's dedicated mission in Mecca that God declared those whom the Prophet had addressed but who had rejected him as 'deniers', and it was then that God revealed this commandment. It is thus impermissible to declare anyone to be a 'denier' or a *kafir* without having engaged in this sort of dedicated, sustained mission as the Prophet did in Mecca. It must be emphasised that it was only after thirteen years of the Prophet's mission in Mecca that God declared certain people or be *kafirs* or deniers, and for ordinary Muslims like us to do so, even a hundred and thirteen years of preaching work will not be adequate.

In some Quranic verses, revealed while the Prophet was in Mecca, there are certain references to non-Muslims living outside Arabia. For instance, the Quran mentions the Romans, who were Christians, over whom the Persians had secured a temporary victory.

But here it refers to them as Romans and not as *kafirs*. Likewise, the Quran refers to the non-Muslim ruler of Yemen, Abraha, but it does not label him as a *kafir* ruler. In contrast, the Quran uses the terms *kafir* and *kufr* with regard to the Quraish of Mecca who denied the Prophet. It did not refer to all non-Muslims as *kafirs*. For instance, when the Prophet migrated to Medina, he did not refer to the people of Medina as *kafirs*, but, rather, as 'people'. There were several non-Muslim tribes living around Medina at that time, but they, too, were not referred to as *kafirs* by the Prophet. Instead, he referred to them by their usual names, such as Ahl-e Saqif ('the people of Saqif'), Ahl-e Najran ('the people of Najran'), Ahl-e Bahrain ('the people of Bahrain'), and so on.

In the same way, in the early Islamic period, soon after the Prophet's demise, when the Arab Muslims spread out of Arabia into other countries, they referred to the non-Muslim communities they encountered by their own names, not as *kafirs*. For example, they called the Christians of Syria as 'Christians' (*Masihi*), the Jews of Palestine as 'Jews' (*Yahud*), the Magians of Iran as 'Magians' (*Majus*), the Buddhists of Afghanistan as 'Buddhists' (*Bodh* or *Boza*), and so on. When the first Muslims landed in India, they did the same. They referred to the non-Muslims of India as *Hindu*s, which is the Arab way of pronouncing the word *Sindhu*. One of the earliest Arab Muslim chroniclers of India, Abu al-Rehan al-Biruni, author of the well-known *Kitab ul-Hind* ('The Book of India'), referred to the non-Muslims of India as *Hindu*s, not as *kafirs*.

Some Historical Instances

As I have discussed earlier, the form of address contained in the Quran 'Say, "You who deny the Truth [...]"' (109:1) applies only to those Meccans who denied the Prophet even after he preached among them for thirteen years and provided them with all the necessary proofs. The Quran does not address anyone else in this specific manner besides these pagans of Mecca of the Prophet's time. After the Prophet's conquest of Mecca, several Arab tribes sent delegations to meet him. For instance, some people came to meet him from Yemen. He addressed them as 'people of Yemen' (Ahl-e Yaman), not as '*kafirs* from Yemen'. Similarly, the Prophet sent letters to the rulers of various lands near Arabia, inviting them to the path of God. He did not refer to them in these letters as *kafirs*.

The investigation of *kufr* with regard to a particular person can happen only after all the necessary proofs of the faith have been presented before him. The model of setting out the proofs (*etemam-e hujjat*) is just one—that is, the thirteen-year-long preaching mission of the Prophet in Mecca. Further, even after one has properly and adequately set out the proofs of the faith, it is only for God to specify, if He wishes a particular person to be a *kafir* or 'denier' of the Truth. We cannot do this ourselves.

Heated Polemics

When the British ruled India, Muslim and Hindu preachers engaged in heated public polemical debates or *munazara*. This took the place of what rightly belonged to *da'wah* or inviting, with love and concern, people to the path of God. These debates contributed in a major way to the rapid worsening of Hindu-Muslim relations across the country.

This is not the Islamic way of approaching people of other faiths. The true Islamic way is through addressing others while being inspired by a spirit of love, compassion and concern for their welfare, in spite of their opposition. In contrast, polemical debates aim at defeating and demeaning others. Instead of love and understanding, they produce only more hate and conflict, thereby creating even more problems.

The Notion of *Dar ul-Da'wah* ('The Abode of Inviting People to the Path of God')

The terms *dar ul-kufr* ('the abode of infidelity') and *bilad al-kuffar* ('the land of the infidels') are not found in the Quran. They are a later invention, which emerged after the demise of the Prophet and date to the Abbasid period. They were not in use among Muslims before this. In my opinion, these terms are not proper. Lands other than those that can, if at all, be called 'Islamic' countries, must be seen and termed as *dar ul-da'wah* or 'abodes of inviting others to the path of God', and these include even those countries that some Muslims might regard as opposed to them.

In the Quran, God addresses the Prophet and instructs him thus:

> *This is a blessed Book which We have revealed, confirming what came before it, so that you may warn the 'Umm al-Quraa [Mother of Cities] and the people around it (6:92).*

The term *'Umm al-Quraa* in this verse refers to the city of Mecca. When this verse was revealed, Mecca was under the control of non-Muslims, so much so that they had installed numerous idols inside the Ka'aba. Despite this, the Quran did not refer to the Mecca of this period as *dar ul-kufr*, but rather, as *'Umm al-Quraa* or 'Mother of Cities', and commanded the Prophet to engage in the work of *da'wah* there. From this one can infer that all places that are under the control of non-Muslims can be considered as *dar ul-da'wah*, thus indicating to Muslims their duty of *da'wah* or inviting to God's path the people of these lands. To refer to them with terms such as *dar ul-kufr* or *bilad al-kuffar* is not proper.

This is a translation of a chapter titled *Kufr Aur Kafir Ka Masla* ('The Issue of *Kufr* and *Kafir*'), in Maulana Wahiduddin Khan's book titled, *Hikmat-e Islam* ('The Wisdom of Islam'), Goodword Books, New Delhi, 2008, pp.35–48.

8

On the Terms *Dar ul-Islam, Dar ul-Kufr,* and *Dar ul-Harb*

Fiqh, or Muslim jurisprudence, is a product of the exercise of human reflection, deduction and *ijtihad*, and is not itself a form of divine knowledge. The development and compilation of the corpus of *fiqh* began after the period of the Prophet Muhammad and his Companions, particularly at the time of the Abbasids. The *ulema* of that period reflected on the Quran and Hadith and developed certain terms on their own. Three key terms in this regard are the following: *dar ul-islam* ('abode of Islam'); *dar ul-kufr* ('abode of infidelity'); and *dar ul-harb* ('abode of war'). The *fuqaha*, scholars of *fiqh*, made further finer distinctions within each of these *dar*s or 'abodes', but here I will consider only these three main terms.

The *fuqaha* who developed these terms in the Abbasid period were regarded by later *ulema* as full-fledged *mujtahids* (*mujtahid-e mutlaq*), scholars qualified to engage in *ijtihad*. That is why for many centuries no scholar raised any question as to the veracity of these terms. However, if examining the terms with an open mind, one realises that they are undoubtedly not in accordance with the spirit of Islam.

It is crucial to note that these terms devised by the medieval *fuqaha* are not present in either the Quran or the Hadith. The *fuqaha* invented these terms using their prerogative of *ijtihad*. There are certain strict rules for proper *ijtihad*, and if these rules are not followed, the *ijtihad* is wrong. That is why the *ulema* agree that the *ijtihad* of a *mujtahid* can be both right as well as wrong.

Ijtihad is a principle of the *shariah*. The *ulema* generally agree that this principle is rooted in a hadith report attributed to Mu'az bin Jabal, a Companion who, when he was sent to Yemen by the Prophet, was asked how he would solve any problem that he faced. He replied that he would do so in accordance with the Quran. The Prophet asked him then, that if the matter was not mentioned in the Quran, what he would do. To that he answered that he would abide in that regard with the Prophet's practice (*sunnah*). The Prophet then asked, if the matter was not dealt with in his *sunnah,* what would he do? Mu'az bin Jabal replied that he would exercise his judgment through *ijtihad*. The Prophet appreciated this reply.

The *ulema* regard this *hadith* report as the basic source and foundation of the principle of *ijtihad*. This *hadith* report indicates very clearly that *ijtihad* is legitimate only when no explicit guidance is available on a particular matter in both the Quran and in the Sunnah of the Prophet. If such guidance is available in either or both of these sources, then *ijtihad* is not permissible. For instance, from the Quran it is evident that the month of fasting is Ramadan, and so there is no possibility of *ijtihad* in deciding the month of fasting. Likewise, the Hadith indicates that the number of compulsory daily prayers is five, and so no one can seek to engage in *ijtihad* in this matter in order to reduce or increase this figure.

Based on this principle, it is apparent that there is clear guidance in the Quran and Sunnah about the conditions denoted by the terms *dar ul-islam, dar ul-kufr,* and *dar-ul harb,* although they do not use these terms. Because of this, it is not proper for any scholar or *faqih* to engage in *ijtihad* to develop new terms to denote these concepts or conditions. Now, the conditions that these three terms devised by the later *fuqaha* describe were present at the time of the Prophet himself. Despite this, the Prophet did not use these terms to denote these conditions. These terms thus cannot be regarded as a result of proper and acceptable *ijtihad*.

The first thirteen years of the Prophet's life in Mecca, from the time he received his prophethood up till his migration to Medina, were characterised by conditions for which the later *fuqaha* invented the term *dar ul-kufr* to describe. Yet, neither the Quran nor the Hadith reports described the Mecca of this period as *dar ul-kufr*. Following the Prophet's migration to Medina, the Meccan pagans launched an open war against him. In other words, the Mecca of this period was characterised by conditions for which the later *fuqaha* invented the term *dar ul-harb*. Yet, neither the Quran nor the Hadith refer to the Mecca of this period as *dar ul-harb*. Following his migration to Medina, the Prophet established a polity, of which he was the head. In other words, the conditions in Medina at this time were those that the later *fuqaha* developed the term *dar ul-islam* to denote. Yet, the Quran did not describe the Medina of that period as *dar ul-islam* and neither did the Prophet.

The Quran refers to heaven as *dar us-salam* or the 'abode of peace' (*Surah Yunus*: 25) but it does not refer to any place on earth as *dar ul-islam* or *dar ul-iman* ('abode of faith'). Likewise, the Quran refers to the place of punishment after death for deniers of the truth as *dar ul-bavar* or the 'abode of loss' (*Surah Ibrahim*: 28), but it does not term any piece of land on earth as *dar ul-kufr* or *dar ul-kuffar* ('abode of infidels'). In other words, the use of the terms *dar ul-islam, dar ul-harb* and *dar ul-kufr,* is not permissible. These terms represent a wrong innovation (*biddat*), rather than being a Prophetic practice (*sunnat*).

It is clear from what I have written that the conditions for which the later *fuqaha* invented the terms *dar ul-islam, dar ul-kufr* and *dar ul-harb* to describe were present at the time of the Prophet at different stages of his life and in different places. Yet these were not referred to at the time of the Prophet by these terms. Under these circumstances, one can rightly argue that in coining these terms, the *fuqaha* of the Abbasid period exceeded the bounds of legitimate *ijtihad*. In other words, they sought to do something for which they did not have the right. It can, therefore, be clearly stated that these terms coined by the *fuqaha* are an instance of erroneous *ijtihad*. Hence, a scholar of Islam is within his rights to reject this *ijtihad*. Since they represent a *biddat*, they must be rejected, for in a *hadith* report the Prophet is said to have exhorted Muslims to reject anything new that might be sought to be added to his faith.

The debate about these three terms is no mere academic or peripheral one. Rather, it is an exceedingly serious issue, for it is inextricably linked to the way in which many Muslims view the world. These terms, needless to say, help create an unwarranted sense among Muslims of being God's 'chosen people'. This sort of mentality is, in fact, a sign of a community's downfall, rather than its eminence, as is clear from the example of the Jews.

It is evident from the Quran that God does not view the world on the basis of, or in terms of, divisions between *dar ul-islam, dar ul-kufr* and *dar ul-harb*. God regards all human beings through one, and only one, perspective. He will deal with human beings after their death based on a single common criterion. In this regard, it is pertinent to note that the Quran sternly forbids people from imagining that they are loved more by God than other people just because they belong to a certain community (*Surah Al-Maida*: 18). The Quran clearly states that in God's eyes, a person's value is determined not on the basis of his communitarian association or race, but rather, on the basis of her or his own actions (*Surah An-Najm*: 39). The Quran brackets Muslims with Jews and Christians and says, 'It will not be in accordance with your desires, nor the desires of the people of the Scriptures. He who doeth wrong will have the recompense thereof, and will not find against Allah any protecting friend or helper' (*Surah An-Nisa*: 123).

In other words, the concept of the superiority of a certain community based on birth is totally alien to the Quran. This is clearly indicated, for instance, in the Quranic verse which says: 'Lo! Those who believe (in that which is revealed unto thee, Muhammad), and those who are Jews, and Christians, and Sabaeans—whoever believeth in Allah and the Last Day and doeth right—surely their reward is with their Lord, and there shall no fear come upon them neither shall they grieve' (*Surah Al-Baqarah*: 62). This means that the Muslim community, the Jewish community or the Christian community are, from the communitarian point of view, the same in God's eyes. Success in the court of God will depend not on one's communitarian affiliation, but rather, on one's actions.

This statement of the Quran indicates, therefore, that the true Islamic perspective is to see the cosmos in terms of God versus humanity, rather than in terms of Muslims versus non-Muslims. The latter way of thinking is a narrow, communal one, and has no relationship with the Quran or Islam. It is against God's creation plan, for God has made this world for all His creatures, and not just for Muslims alone. This is why, in the light of the Quran, if the concept of *dar* or abode is to be used, it can be said that the entire world is *dar ul-insan* or 'abode of humanity'.

Because of the way of imagining the world on the basis of the three *dars* that the medieval *fuqaha* had devised, Muslims began to see things in a narrow, sectarian way, in terms of Muslims versus 'others'. As a result, Muslims began relating to human history simply from their own reference point. They started classifying people from their own narrow point of view, considering themselves as one, and all others as belonging to the community of *kafirs*. They considered all fellow Muslims as their own, and the rest as 'others', as *kafirs* and as potential or real enemies. They wrongly thought that all the good news that the Quran talks of referred to them alone, and that the punishments that it speaks of applied to the rest of humanity.

This way of imagining and dividing humankind that Muslims have devised is totally against the Quran. The Quran clearly indicates that it classifies and categorises humankind with reference to God. In contrast, the concept of the *dars* as developed by the *fuqaha* divided humankind with reference to Muslims, into two conflicting categories: Muslims and non-Muslims. This way of looking at humankind is now deep-rooted among Muslims. This is why almost all the books penned by Muslim scholars that describe Muslim history after the period of the Prophet reflect what can be called a Muslim-centric approach. The only exception to this rule that I can think of is the well-known *Muqaddima* or 'Introduction' to world history by Abdur Rahman Ibn Khaldun, which is the only work of a Muslim historian that I know of that reflects a humanity-oriented approach. Likewise, and because of this adversarial mentality—in which the concept of the *dars* as developed by the later *fuqaha* has played a major role in promoting—almost all books written by Muslim scholars seeking to address non-Muslims have taken the form of heated polemics, giving the impression that the generality of humankind is not a matter of particular concern for Muslims. This is indeed very lamentable and unfortunate.

The commentaries that were written by later Islamic scholars on the Quran and Hadith also could not escape the influence of the notion of the *dars* that the Abbasid *fuqaha* had developed. Thus, for instance, the Quran uses the term *khair-e ummat* (Surah Al-e Imran: 110). Later Quranic commentators took this to be synonymous with the Muslim community as a whole, as indicating that the Muslim community in its entirety was the best among all communities. However, it is clear that this is not the intention of the Quran, which refers in this verse not to a group based on birth, but rather, to a collectivity based on their personal virtues, good attributes, and actions.

The same communitarian prejudices which the concept of the *dars* had given such a boost to are evident in the work of numerous later Hadith commentators as well. For instance, it is reported in the *Sahih* of al-Bukhari that once, in Medina, a funeral procession carrying a corpse passed by the Prophet, who was at that moment sitting down. On seeing this he got up. When he was told that it was the funeral ceremony of a Jew, he replied, 'Was he not a human being?'

This action of the Prophet clearly tells us that every human being is worthy of respect and regard, irrespective of her or his religion. Seeing another person, no matter what his or her religion should be, reminds everyone that just as God has created oneself, He has created others as well, and one should then marvel at the miracle of God's creation. Thinking in this way on seeing another human being is thus a means for seeking to understand God.

The above example undoubtedly illustrates the Prophet's practice of respect for all humankind. Yet it is strange that no Hadith commentators understood this incident to mean this way. What they have done instead is to cook up strange explanations for this event. Some claimed that the Prophet's standing up was not compulsory or necessary (*wajib*). Others argued that he stood up in fear of death, or that this action of his was just an impulsive reaction. Still others wrote that he stood up out of respect for the angel that was walking along with the corpse or for the angel of death (*malak ul-maut*). Some claim that he stood up out of irritation with the incense that accompanied the corpse, or that he did so in order that the corpse would not pass higher than his head. Some say that although he stood up, this commandment or practice was later abrogated and no longer applies to Muslims. And so have their explanations gone.

I believe that all these explanations are incorrect. Because of their peculiar mental make-up, however, these Hadith commentators did not even realise that the interpretations that they were giving were, God forbid, belittling the Prophet's Sunnah. Such tradition of negative sentiments about non-Muslims continues even today, through the Muslim media and through the vast number of books that Muslim scholars are producing, which have sought to fortify this communal mindset of Muslims but which have no positive attraction for or appeal to non-Muslims.

Let me refer to a recent instance in this regard. Some time back, a 'Quran Television' channel, known as QTV, was launched in a certain Muslim country, and it has proven to be immensely popular among Muslims. Although this channel was launched in the name of the Quran, in fact it has only served to provide fodder to the particular psyche of Muslim communitarianism. It does not address non-Muslim minds. In reality, it is a television channel of and for the Muslim community, and not really 'Quran TV', as it claims to be.

Not long ago, the noted Indian writer Khushwant Singh penned an article titled *Spreading Islamophobia*, where he argued:

> *About the most disturbing phenomenon of the past decade is the widening divide between the Islamic and non-Islamic world [...] I looked forward to the Pakistani channel QTV to take the lead in this direction. I made it a point to tune in every afternoon to see and hear how it was going about its mission. I was sorely disappointed. I expected it would address itself to non-Muslim audiences, among which wrong notions about Islam persist. I found it focused entirely on Muslims to assure them that their faith was better than any other and that anyone who disagreed is an ignoramus.*

What Khushwant Singh has written actually applies to almost every Muslim writer and orator. This Muslim-centric mentality, which came into being after the Prophet, is the sole reason why the Muslims completely forgot their mission of *da'wah* or inviting others to the faith. This Muslim-oriented or Muslim-centric thinking makes Muslims 'Muslim-friendly', while humanity-oriented thinking, which the Quran prescribes, should have made Muslims 'humanity-friendly'. But because Muslims adopted a narrow communitarian mindset vis-à-vis others, in contrast to what the Quran expected from them, they began to focus simply on their own communitarian concerns rather than on their actual mission of *da'wah*.

This approach and way of thinking has been continuing for a long time now. It is, as discussed earlier, deeply rooted in the work of classical *fiqh* that developed in the Abbasid period, and that continue to be looked at as sources of guidance. Literally thousands of books have so far been penned on the subject of *fiqh*, but these are completely bereft of any chapters related to da'wah and tabligh, or communicating the faith to others. Unfortunately, reflecting the notion of the *dar*s as devised by the latter-day *fuqaha*, non-Muslims were treated simply as objects or targets of armed jihad by Muslims in the later *fiqh* literature, and not as people who should be invited with kindness to the path of God.

A result of this wholly erroneous way of thinking was that Muslims fell victim to a deadening intellectual stagnation and, at the same time, emerged as enemies of other communities. The relationship between Muslims and others should have been one between missionaries of the faith (*da'i*) and addressees (*mad'u*); this was completely overturned and they both began to see each other as inveterate foes.

The later *fuqaha* who devised the notions of the *dar*s believed that any land could either be *dar ul-islam* or *dar ul-harb*. Some of them even went to the extent of claiming that if in a country ruled by a non-Muslim government Muslims were allowed to follow the prescriptions of Islam, it would still be considered as *dar ul-harb*. If these *fuqaha* had any consciousness of the need for, and duty of, da'wah and tabligh, they would have realised that such a country could have been categorised instead as *dar ul-da'wah* or 'abode of da'wah'.

The term *dar ul-harb* is seen as offensive by non-Muslims. Especially in today's age, Muslims cannot live in a balanced and harmonious way if they carry about in their heads the mental baggage represented by the term *dar ul-harb*. The classical *fuqaha* could only think of the world in terms of *dar ul-islam* and *dar ul-harb*, but, as I said, if they had truly understood the imperative of Islamic *da'wah*, they could have easily realised that other lands should be considered as places where *da'wah* work needed to be done by Muslims, and hence could have categorised them as *dar ul-da'wah*. Spaces and opportunities for *da'wah* always exist in every country, and even if a country becomes as fiercely opposed to Islam as Mecca was in the first years of the Prophet's mission it will still remain as *dar ul-da'wah*. No country, no matter what its conditions, can cease being *dar ul-da'wah*, as is evident from the history of the prophets as mentioned in the Quran.

Thus the fact of the matter is that the entire world, in the sense of being home to all human beings, can be considered as *dar ul-insan* or 'abode of humanity', and, from the point of view of Islamic mission, as *dar ul-da'wah*. Those countries that are commonly thought of as *dar ul-islam* can, in fact, be considered as *dar ul-muslimin* or 'abode of Muslims' but not truly as *dar ul-islam*.

The Quran refers to the Prophet as a 'sincere and trustworthy adviser' (*nasih*) (*Surah Al-Araf*: 68). That is to say that while the Prophet is an adviser or *nasih*, the people he addresses are *mansuh* or those whose real welfare should be promoted. In other words, the relation between them is that of a *da'i* and *mad'u*, addresser or inviter to the faith, and addressee. Because the Prophet Muhammad was the seal of the prophets, after him his followers are required to shoulder this responsibility of *da'wah* and guidance. That is to say, the relationship between Muslims and others should be that of *nasih* and *mansuh*, or *da'i* and *mad'u*. This relationship points to the need for Muslims to possess and reflect a certain moral character and values. To be effective *da'is* of the faith demands that Muslims must relate with positive virtues to others, irrespective of how the latter might behave with them. Even if they have to suffer torments at the hands of the latter, they must never give up patience and determination in order to maintain the climate needed for *da'wah.*

This characteristic of *da'wah* must be preserved at all costs, by ordinary Muslims, Muslim governments and their officials, Muslim political parties and their leaders, the Muslim media, and Muslims in all other spheres of society, including the *ulema.* It must be realised that the tradition of *fiqh* that devised the concepts of the three *dars* has done great damage in this regard and has fanned hatred in the hearts of Muslims against other peoples. It must also be understood that since Islam requires its followers to address others with its message, they should have no hatred or complaint against the latter in their capacity of being potential addressees of the Divine message. This is a very serious issue that requires a critical re-examination. Nothing less will do.

This task is undoubtedly difficult. Muslims today number over a billion, and there are many commercial or vested interests involved that want to maintain the status quo and exploit religion for worldly ends. They seek to stoke the emotions of Muslim communalism to promote these nefarious purposes. This makes it an immensely difficult task to re-examine our ways of looking at the world and at relating to other communities.

We urgently need a true revival in our way of understanding the world, ourselves, and others. According to a *hadith* report, the Prophet Muhammad said that after him if anyone revived a practice or *sunnat* of his that had gone into neglect, he would receive the reward of a hundred martyrs. This means that reviving a lost Prophetic practice is as major and daunting a task as the sacrifice of a hundred martyrs. And one such practice and task that needs to be revived is that of proper *da'wah*. This task requires in-depth study and knowledge, far-sightedness, wisdom, planning, patience and determination. Without all these, this task will fail.

Another such task is what is termed *tajdid-e din* or 'revival of the faith'. This project of revival requires that certain deeply-rooted notions in Muslims' minds be extirpated. It is a form of de-conditioning of conditioned mindsets or a re-processing of history. It requires the overcoming of a thousand years of history in order to return to the first period of Islam, the time of the Prophet, and to fashion the framework of Islamic knowledge on the pattern of that period. This is undoubtedly an immensely crucial task before the Muslim *ummah*. Those who have taken up this task will have to make huge sacrifices.

This is a translation of a chapter titled *Dar ul-Islam, Dar ul-Kufr, Dar ul-Harb*, in Maulana Wahiduddin Khan's book, *Hikmat-e Islam* ('The Wisdom of Islam'), Goodword Books, New Delhi, 2008, pp. 22–34.

9
Pakistani Terrorists' Anti-Indian and Anti-Islamic Rhetoric

Pakistan-based radical Islamist groups such as the Lashkar-e Tayyeba and the Jaish-e Muhammad often refer to a saying attributed to the Prophet Muhammad in which, so they claim, the Prophet is said to have prophesied a battle against India, the *ghazwat ul-hind*, that would be fought by a group of Muslims who would be saved from the fires of hell. This alleged *hadith* is routinely used by these groups as a major tool for recruitment and to justify war against India, which they describe as a jihad, promising their fighters that this would guarantee them a place in heaven.

There are many books of Hadith, and this report is contained in just one of them—in the collection by Imam al-Nasai. According to this report, the Prophet is claimed to have declared that God has saved two groups from among his followers from the fires of hell. The first group would consist of those who participate in the *ghazwat ul-hind* and the second would be those who would be with Jesus at the time of his Second Coming.

Groups like the Lashkar deliberately twist the term *ghazwat ul-hind* to give it a wrong meaning, claiming that it refers to a violent war to be waged against India by some Muslims. They translate the word *ghazwa* to mean a physical war. Actually, the original and literal meaning of the word is simply 'to move or to shift from one place to another'. In the more contemporary period of Muslim history, however, the term came to be used synonymously with violent war, or what is also known as *qital* in Arabic. This is how the term *ghazwat ul-hind* is misinterpreted by terrorist groups such as the Lashkar.

I do not agree with this interpretation at all. The word *ghazwa* can be interpreted to simply mean a campaign with a mission, without necessarily connoting any form of violence. I interpret the term to mean a peaceful missionary campaign or what is called *da'wah* in Arabic. The early books of *sirah* or biographies of the Prophet describe more than eighty of what they call *ghazwa*s, and of these, only three involved actual fighting or war—the *ghazwa*s of Badr, Uhud, and Hunain. The rest were intended to be peaceful missionary tours or campaigns consisting of delegations of Muslims, sometimes led by the Prophet, to various non-Muslim tribes. In some cases, these missionaries were attacked by their opponents and there were minor skirmishes when Muslims had to resort to self-defence, but in many cases this did not happen at all. All these are also termed as *ghazwa*s in the early biographies of the Prophet.

This being the case, I would interpret the *hadith* about the *ghazwat ul-hind* to mean that a group of Muslims would engage in peaceful missionary work in India, bringing the message of monotheism to this country. In my view, it is certainly not the violent hate-driven war that groups like the Lashkar say it is.

This *hadith* has also to be considered along with another *hadith*, which, quite predictably, groups like the Lashkar conveniently never quote, in which the Prophet is said to have declared that he felt 'cool breeze of knowledge coming from the land of India' (*ajedo rih al-ilm min bilad al-hind*). This can be interpreted to mean that the Prophet believed that one day India would become a great source of spiritual knowledge.

If this *hadith* is seen in conjunction with the *hadith* about the *ghazwat ul-hind*, it can be interpreted to mean that a group of true believers would engage in peaceful missionary work in India, after which spiritual knowledge would spread out from India to other lands. This would be the absolute opposite of the explanation of the *ghazwat ul-hind* being pronounced by radical groups like the Lashkar.

It must be noted that there is no consensus among the *ulema* on the veracity of this *hadith*. Generally, those *hadith* reports that have multiple chains of narrators, or what are called *khabar-e mutawatir*, are considered by the ulema to be sound, while those that have just one narrator, or *khabar-e wahid*, are often seen as weak (*za'if*), suspect or dubious, and sometimes even completely fabricated (*mauzu*). It is crucial to note that this narration about the *ghazwat ul-hind* has just one narrator. As such, its veracity—or, otherwise, falsity—must further be gauged by taking into account the fact that besides Imam al-Nasai's collection, no other collection of Hadith reports contains this narration.

There are varying opinions among Muslim scholars about the reliability or validity of various *hadith* reports, and even about the very corpus of Hadith itself. Some scholars reject the entire corpus of Hadith, saying it is unreliable and insisting that the only source of guidance should be the Quran. The majority of the *ulema*, however, consider the corpus of Hadith to also be a source of guidance. At the same time, many of them point out that several *hadith* reports, including some that are found in what the Sunnis regard as authoritative collections (*sihah sitta*), such as that by Imam Bukhari and Imam Muslim, are weak, unreliable, or fabricated.

I do not want to get into the question of whether or not the report about the *ghazwat ul-hind* is true or fabricated, because obviously, different Muslim ideologues have different opinions about the matter. My point is that this *hadith* must be interpreted in the manner that I have done above, because that is precisely what I believe is in accordance with the teachings of the Quran. A generally accepted principle among the *ulema* is that if a *hadith* report or its interpretation goes against the Quran, it must be rejected. Since the Lashkar's interpretation of the *hadith* about the *ghazwat ul-hind* is a complete violation of the Quran and what it teaches about how people of other faiths should be related to, this interpretation must be rejected outright.

The Quran specifically mentions that there is to be no compulsion in religious matters. It says that Muslims must seek to convey God's message to others through love and in a peaceful manner, not through force. Moreover, even if others choose not to accept this message, they should be left in peace. Unfortunately, some radical, misguided so-called Islamic groups wrongly claim that Muslims must offer non-Muslims either Islam or death. This is completely absurd.

Unlike what groups like the Lashkar wrongly argue, there is no room for offensive war in Islam. Islam allows only for war in self-defence, and that, too, only in cases of clear aggression and after all methods of peaceful negotiation have been tried and have failed. This is yet another reason why I firmly believe that the Lashkar's interpretation of the narration about the *ghazwat ul-hind* is absolutely wrong.

Another fact that must be noted in this regard is that there is a consensus among the *ulema* that declaring war is the prerogative of only an established State, or as it is expressed in Arabic, *ar-rahil li al-imam*. This means that in Islam all other forms of war are illegitimate or *haram*, including terrorism and proxy war, such as that which groups like the Lashkar are engaged in. They are nothing more than a bunch of rabble-rousers. There are no reliable *ulema* among them. Their claims to speak on behalf of Islam are absolutely untenable.

Self-styled Islamist groups, like the Lashkar, represent a certain ideology; obviously, to counter them, we need a counter-ideology. We have to present and propagate the true Islamic ideology to defeat these groups who are misinterpreting Islam for their own nefarious purposes. A simple military solution cannot suffice. In places like Assam or Sri Lanka, ongoing violent movements are mainly about politics, power, or land, and hence can be solved by addressing these issues. But radical Islamist movements are, to a great extent, motivated by purely ideological—as opposed to simply material—concerns. This means that a powerful counter-ideology has to be devised to defeat them. They cannot be defeated simply by bombing their training areas.

Hatred and militancy lay at the very basis of the Pakistan demand, and so, in a sense, what is being witnessed in that country today, including the emergence and spread of terrorist groups like the Lashkar, is a logical culmination of the hate-driven and utterly baseless 'two nation' theory of the pre-Partition Muslim League. The political interpretation of Islam that groups like the Lashkar propagate is an illegitimate innovation, or what is called *biddah* in Arabic, a relatively recent invention, dating back to the early twentieth century. The two principal inventors of this ideology were the Egyptian Syed Qutb and the Pakistani ideologue Abul Ala Maududi, the founder of the Jama'at-e Islami. They were the ones who concocted the theory that Muslims are like a political party that must constantly struggle, using violence if need be, to rise up against existing systems and establish what they called an Islamic State. They were the ones who first conceived the term and concept of Islam as a 'complete ideology' or 'complete system', or *nizam-e shamil* as it is called in Arabic or *nizam-e kamil* in Urdu. Before this, these terms were never used by Islamic scholars. These two ideologues claimed that those Muslims who did not agree with this theory were not true Muslims at all. That effectively meant that they considered that the many Muslim scholars and Sufis before them, starting from the Abbasid period onwards, who did not advocate this sort of radicalism, had departed from what they imagined was the true Islam. From this you can see what a major deviation in Islamic thought Islamist ideologues like Maududi and Qutb, and present-day groups like the Lashkar, actually represent.

This is a translation of the transcript of an interview given to Yoginder Sikand by Maulana Wahiduddin Khan in New Delhi on 5 February 2008.

10

Understanding Extremism in the Name of Islam

In order to understand the numerous conflicts in much of the Muslim world today, it is crucial to remember that at one time the Muslims had a vast Empire, stretching from Spain in the west to India and beyond in the east. All these territories then came under European colonial rule. The Muslim intellectuals of that time, however, failed to properly respond to the European challenge. They did not give their society the sort of leadership that was required. They saw European colonialism in terms of an anti-Muslim conspiracy, a mere replay of the Crusades. They bitterly criticised the Europeans as enemies of Islam. But that, I feel, was a completely wrong explanation of the European success. Actually, it is one of the laws of history that at one time a certain power becomes dominant, only to eventually fade away and make way for the emergence of another power. In India there were the Rajas, then the Mughals came, and finally the British. Then India became independent, and even now you sometimes have the Congress and sometimes the Bharatiya Janata Party.

The way I see it, the Europeans were able to conquer the Muslim world not because of any anti-Islamic conspiracy but simply because of their technological superiority. We Muslims knew of water only as water, or at most, we used it to propel water mills to grind flour. The Europeans, on the other hand, went ahead and used water to generate steam power. We fought with swords but they used guns; naturally, they were victorious. Lamentably, the Muslim intellectuals of the last hundred years, and even today, generally saw, and continue to see, European and now American superiority in terms of a so-called grand anti-Islamic conspiracy. This explains, to a great extent, the seemingly never-ending cycles of violence in much of the Muslim world even today. This hatred for all other people that is drilled into the minds of ordinary Muslims gives reason enough to fear.

When I was a child, I was taught to believe that the British were wholly evil and that nothing good could be attributed to them. It was only later that I discovered the many good things that they had done in India, such as building modern schools and the railways. I think if our intellectuals had told us that the decline of Muslim power had nothing to do with any so-called anti-Islamic conspiracy but that it was mainly because of the West's technological superiority, we would not have had the sort of militancy that we are witnessing today.

If you look at the sort of so-called Islamic literature that has flooded the market you will see that most Muslim writers continue to propagate the so-called conspiracy theory, branding non-Muslims as evil enemies of Islam, whose only mission in life is, so they allege, to destroy Islam and the Muslims. Some days ago, I got a letter from somebody in Kashmir who said that till recently, he had been only exposed to the writings of the militant so-called Islamists. He wrote that because of this, he had been led to believe that all Hindus—and all non-Muslims in general—were the sworn enemies of the Muslims. He then added that he had come across some of my books which had undoubtedly transformed the way he saw the world. He said that he had experienced a complete change of heart and that he now realises that Hindus, too, are God's children who deserve to be loved.

In this regard, I wish to state that inter-religious dialogue between Muslims and others is today absolutely indispensable, and Islam insists upon it. After all, wherever progress has occurred in history it has been because of interaction between different peoples. This must start right from the school level. Some Muslim clerics say that if children are taught about other religions they will turn away from Islam. But is their faith in Islam so weak that if they hear the truth about other religions they will renounce their own? Islam is not a glass vessel which can easily break into pieces! It is as strong as an iron vessel. We really must get to know the truth about each other's religions and clear up our mutual misunderstandings, because most prejudice is based upon simple ignorance or misrepresentation. As far as Islam is concerned, inter-religious dialogue is a binding duty according to the Quran. In his last pilgrimage to Mecca, the Prophet addressed thousands of his followers and told them to travel all over the world to spread Islam. They went to various countries to preach Islam. It was, however, only one aspect of their work. They also journeyed in search of knowledge, interacting and engaging in open discussions with people of other religions. For example, some of the early Muslims came to India. Here they studied Sanskrit and translated many Sanskrit texts into Arabic. Or, for that matter, when Spain was under Muslim control many Christians would go there to study even the Bible from Muslim scholars.

As part of this inter-religious dialogue project, *madrasa* students, or would-be *ulema*, should be exposed to other religions. The *ulema* must also get involved in inter-religious dialogue work. Some *maulvis* attached to a few *madrasas* have attempted to start dialogue efforts, regularly inviting secular Hindu intellectuals to seminars and conferences. Sadly, these efforts are not really cutting much ice because they interact with what I call the 'no-problem' Hindus, people who are already convinced of the need for Hindu-Muslim dialogue and understanding. We should try to reach out instead to the 'problem' Hindus, those who are vehemently opposed to Muslims. That is what I have been trying to do, for which many Muslims have bitterly opposed me. Actually, I have found that many Hindus are anti-Muslim simply because of their ignorance or misunderstanding of Islam, and that once you begin to dialogue with them and explain to them what Islam is all about, they begin to shed their prejudices.

This is a translation of the transcript of an interview transcript given to Yoginder Sikand by Maulana Wahiduddin Khan in New Delhi on 3 December 2004.

11
Ijtihad, Freedom of Expression, and Jihad

uslims today suffer from a bizarre sense of loss. Perhaps no other community faces this sort of predicament to the same extent. They have failed to make use of the myriad opportunities provided by modernity; one of these valuable opportunities is freedom. The ideologues of the French Revolution claimed that man is born free but everywhere is in chains. This became the slogan of the modern world, and now freedom has been accepted as the basic right of every human being. Everyone has the right to adopt what he or she thinks is right and to act accordingly. There is only one limit to this unfettered freedom: in the exercise of one's right one should not harm someone else, and in the pursuit of one's objectives one should seek to use peaceful, not violent, means.

Three hundred or so years ago, when Amserica won freedom from England, an American man, so the story goes, rushed out into the street to celebrate. He swung his arms up in the air in glee and, as he brought them down, he hit the nose of a passerby. The latter was, naturally, enraged, and demanded an apology. The first man said to him, 'Now America is free and so I can do what I want.' The passerby retorted, 'Undoubtedly you are free, but your freedom ends where my nose begins.'

This story very succinctly expresses the modern concept of democracy. Modernity provides us with freedom but on the condition that the exercise of this freedom does not entail violence against others. Mahatma Gandhi was aware of this principle and used it in the course of the Indian freedom movement. In 1857, Muslim leaders launched a violent movement to oust the British from India, and Muslim-led militant anti-British uprisings continued thereafter for sixty years. However, all these efforts failed. In 1919, Gandhi took over the leadership of the anti-colonial movement and changed its very nature to that of a non-violent struggle, and, finally, India became independent in 1947.

What was the cause of the different fates met by these violent and non-violent movements? One major factor was that the Muslim leaders referred to above were conditioned by a *taqlidi* mindset, blindly adhering to the prescriptions of the established corpus of *fiqh*, and so they knew of only one method of struggle—that of armed jihad. The books of medieval *fiqh* have no conception of peaceful struggle. They speak of just one method—that of violent struggle, because they were written in a period when the only form of power that people knew of was that of the sword. This is reflected in the Arabic saying, 'War can only be stopped by war', and in the Persian phrase, 'Coins are struck in the name of he who wields the sword'.

This militant mindset remains deeply ingrained among most Muslims even today. Hardly any Muslims are free of it. This belief is expressed in different forms. The mental framework which is based on medieval *fiqh* is so deeply entrenched that even many so-called modern Muslim thinkers were and are influenced by it, including Syed Jamaluddin Afghani, Syed Qutb, Muhammad Iqbal, Syed Abul Ala Maududi, and so on. This is the single major cause for the sacrifices of our leaders all going to waste.

The efficacy of non-violent, as opposed to violent, methods in today's world can be understood from an instance from Gandhi's life. Gandhi joined the Indian freedom struggle in 1919. Prior to this, the movement was characterised by violent mobilisation, and the British responded to quash it by counter-violence. When Gandhi announced that the movement would abide by non-violence, the British were confounded, because they had no moral argument to suppress a non-violent freedom movement. It is said that in the wake of Gandhi's announcement, a British collector sent a telegram to his superior officials, saying, 'Kindly wire instructions as to how to kill a tiger non-violently.'

An Anachronistic Approach

Because of their *taqlidi* mindset, present-day Muslim leaders and intellectuals display what can be called an anachronistic approach. The *ulema* of the past who they strictly follow, because of being wedded to the notion of *taqlid*, had no conception of peaceful methods or peaceful struggle. This conception was, admittedly, clearly evident in the Quran and Hadith, but to directly derive rules from the Quran and Hadith *ijtihad* was needed, but the medieval Muslims had already firmly closed the doors of *ijtihad*.

The Quran describes an eternal law in the following words: 'such settlement is best' (*Surah Al-Nisa*: 128). This means that the method of adjustment, reconciliation and making peace is better than the confrontational approach. This clearly indicates the importance of non-violence as compared to violence. Likewise, according to a *hadith* report, the Prophet is said to have declared that God gives in response to softness that which he does not give in response to harshness. This clearly means that peaceful methods are more efficacious than violent ones. Lamentably, although the Quran and Hadith contain such explicit teachings in support of peaceful methods, modern-day Muslim leaders and intellectuals, owing to their *taqlidi* approach, failed to discern these teachings. Instead, they uselessly engaged in conflict and imagined that they were, in this way, setting great examples of sacrifice and martyrdom.

This *taqlidi* mindset has caused considerable harm and destruction to the Muslims themselves, without bringing them any gain whatsoever. If the Palestinians knew this, they would not have unleashed a destructive and violent movement after 1948. Instead, using peaceful methods, they would have made use of the opportunities that were available to them. In that way, they could have gained that position of strength in Palestine that the Jews have acquired in America by using peaceful means and taking advantage of the opportunities opened up by modernity. Likewise, if the Muslims of Kashmir had realised this, they would not have resorted to violent struggle. Using peaceful means, they could have gained such an influential position in India that would have been a hundred times more beneficial for the people of the so-called 'Azad Kashmir'. In the same way, if Muslim leaders in various countries who are engaged in violent movements in order to capture political power had adopted peaceful means, they could have transformed their countries in the direction of truly Islamic societies. But this they could not do, and by resorting to violence instead, they have caused massive destruction to their own people.

The way to win other people's hearts is through promotion of close, peaceful social interaction. In this way, one can influence others through one's morals and personal example. It was this that drew the Quraish pagans towards Islam in the wake of the treaty of Hudaibiyah. On the other hand, promoting conflict with others can only further reinforce their hatred and opposition. But only those with an *ijtihadi* mindset can truly appreciate this fact.

Criticism and Ijtihad

Criticism and *taqlid* are the opposites of each other. Where *taqlid* reigns, there can be no criticism. On the contrary, where criticism is allowed, *taqlid* cannot reign. The matter with *ijtihad* is the opposite of this. *Ijtihad* requires criticism. Where criticism is not allowed, *ijtihad* cannot emerge.

Criticism is not a bad thing *per se*. Rather it is a means for intellectual development. Without criticism, intellectual advancement is not possible. The choice before us is not one between criticism and the lack of it, but, rather, between criticism and intellectual stagnation. If criticism is stopped, our intellectual progress shall also cease.

Ijtihad proceeds through discussion and exchange of views. It is a process of moving from what is known to what is as yet unknown. When we are faced with some problems or issues that need to be answered and if we are free to express our views on them, naturally out of this exchange, new aspects or dimensions of the issues will emerge. This will lead to the clearing up of doubts, and the emergence of a well-researched opinion or position on issues, which is the objective of our intellectual quest. This intellectual activity is known as *ijtihad*.

Ijtihad appears, from both the ideological as well as practical points of view, to be indispensable in life. It is the means for the progress of human communities. A community that does not allow for *ijtihad* will cease to progress. Proper *ijtihad*, as discussed earlier, cannot happen in the absence of the freedom to criticise. Only those who are able to take or accept criticism can benefit from *ijtihad*; people who are unwilling or unable to accept criticism cannot benefit from it.

Let me refer to two illustrations. The battle of Badr took place in the second year of the Islamic century. The Prophet was then in Medina, and he heard that the army of the Quraish was advancing on the town. Accordingly, he gathered his forces and moved in the direction from where the Quraish were coming. He and his Companions halted at a place before Badr. Had they stayed on there, they would have confronted the Quraish army at that spot. A Companion of the Prophet, Khabab bin Manzar, approached the Prophet and asked him if he had chosen to halt at that place because God had instructed him to do so or because he had decided this on his own. The Prophet replied that this was his own opinion. In response, Khabab bin Manzar said that the place was not appropriate.

Now, this response might appear as a sort of criticism. However, the Prophet did not take this in a negative manner, but simply asked Khabab bin Manzar why he did not feel that the place was appropriate to halt at. In reply, this Companion of the Prophet noted that there were several wells located between the Muslims and the Quraish army. If the Muslims halted at that spot, it would allow the Quraish to capture the wells. He, therefore, suggested that they should move ahead till they had gone beyond all the wells and then make a halt. This would cut off the water supply to the enemy army. Hearing this, the Prophet said that Khabab bin Manzar was indeed dispensing sound advice.

This entire conversation between the Prophet and Khabab bin Manzar was conducted in a very balanced way. In the end, the Prophet accepted Khabab bin Manzar's opinion and acted accordingly. And the Muslims won a decisive victory in the battle.

The example clearly indicates how important freedom of expression is for arriving at a proper position. It shows how, through exchanging different, even contradictory, views, new aspects and dimensions of problems can be highlighted, and how this is necessary to come to a proper decision on a particular matter. In fact, so invaluable is this that even if a conflict of opinions becomes heated and aggressive, it must still be cheerfully accepted.

The Harm of Not Accepting Criticism

In 1831, Syed Ahmad Shahid Barelvi gathered an army of Muslims and launched a jihad against Maharaja Ranjit Singh, the Sikh ruler of Punjab. The two armies met at a place called Balakot, and in this battle Syed Ahmad and most of his companions were slain. And so this zealous jihad ended in complete failure.

Most of the men in Syed Ahmad Shahid Barelvi's army were those who had taken an oath of spiritual allegiance to him. One of these men was Maulana Mir Mahbub Ali of Delhi, who was considered to be an accomplished Islamic scholar. He was part of the army of Syed Ahmad Shahid that was advancing to meet the forces of Ranjit Singh. When this army reached a place called Charsaddah, he asked Syed Ahmad on what basis he had declared jihad against the Sikhs. Syed Ahmad replied that he had done so on the basis of divine illumination or *kashf* and dreams that he claimed to have seen. Maulana Mir Mahbub Ali responded that jihad could not be declared on these bases. He cited the Quran as mentioning the need for conducting affairs by mutual consultation (*Surah Al-Shura:* 38). He also added that the Prophet engaged in jihad on the basis of consulting his followers. Hence, he argued, Syed Ahmad should do the same, and that, before launching a jihad, must properly study the then prevailing conditions.

However, Syed Ahmad Shahid did not accept his advice. Instead, he accused him of creating hurdles in his path with his criticism. He told him that his role as his follower was to silently accept what he was told—to be, in fact, as silent as the mountain ahead of them. Maulana Mir Mahbub Ali then left Syed Ahmad's army and returned to Delhi.

This incident is presented in some books of Syed Ahmad Shahid's supporters as a case of Mir Mahbub Ali allegedly having gone astray. Maulana Syed Abdul Haye, former rector of the Nadwat ul-Ulema in Lucknow, wrote that Maulana Mir Mahbub Ali was a great Islamic scholar of his time, but that 'the devil had put an evil suggestion in his heart' and so he abandoned Syed Ahmad Shahid and returned to India.

However, the fact of the matter is that Syed Ahmad Shahid Barelvi did not consult others about the step that he was taking. He did not even investigate the veracity of reports that he had heard about the disrespect of the *shariah* at the hands of the Sikhs in Punjab. Nor did he try to gauge the strength of Maharaja Ranjit Singh's army and find out how his untrained forces could fight it. Instead, he simply entered Ranjit Singh's territory without even proper knowledge of its geographical conditions. Naturally, then, he and most of his companions were easily killed by Ranjit Singh's army. And so his movement ended with a one-sided orgy of destruction that the Muslims had to face.

From this example, one can discern the importance of different and often conflicting, viewpoints in order to arrive at a proper position on collective affairs. People's criticism should be heartily listened to, and only after free intellectual debate and discussion can efforts to reach a proper decision succeed. This, in turn, is related to the need for reviving *ijtihad* at the same time as it points to the hazards of remaining wedded to *taqlid*.

This is a translation of an excerpt of a chapter titled *Taqlid Aur Ijtihad* ('*Taqlid* and *Ijtihad*') in Maulana Wahiduddin Khan's book *Din-o-Shariat: Din-e Islam Ka Ek Fikri Muta'ala* ('Religion and the *Shariah*: An Intellectual Study of the Religion of Islam'), Goodword Books, New Delhi, 2003, pp. 228–240.

12
The Need for Reviving *Ijtihad* Today

Ijtihad is not a mere intellectual exercise. Rather, it is an extremely important and basic requirement for the followers of Islam. Through *ijtihad*, Muslims have been able to re-establish their religious status in every age. Through *ijtihad*, they have also been able to engage in *tatbiq* or reconstructing and reapplying the principles of Islam in accordance with the Quran and Hadith in the context of changing social contexts and conditions, thereby proving that Islam is a religion for all times and that it is as relevant for the future as it was in the past. In other words, *ijtihad* is a means to constantly update Islamic thought and thereby maintain its relevance.

What is *Ijtihad*?

Ijtihad does not mean making decisions or coming to conclusions based on free will. Rather, it denotes reflecting on the primary sources of Islam—the Quran and the Sunnah of the Prophet—and, through deduction (*istinbat*) or analogy (*qiyas*), to suggest rules for new issues and problems. In fact, *ijtihad* is also a form of taqlid. Ordinary *muqallids* do *taqlid* of the learned jurisprudents or *fuqaha*, while a *mujtahid*, one who engages in *ijtihad*, does *taqlid* of God and the Prophet. Examining the Quran and Hadith directly, he deduces rules and guidelines from these sources for issues not explicitly mentioned therein.

By *ijtihad* is meant precisely that intellectual activity which is termed *istinbat* or *qiyas* in the language of the *fuqaha*. This is to say that *ijtihad* is to deduce the rules as regards issues that are not explicitly mentioned in the Quran and Hadith. The term *istinbat* comes from the root *nabt*, which means 'to draw out water from below the ground'. Thus, the term *istinbat al-fiqhiyya* means that a *faqih* or Islamic jurisprudent has closely studied the Quran and Hadith and has revealed its hidden meaning on a particular issue. The noted Quranic commentator al-Qurtabi writes that *istinbat* is the same as *istikhraj* or 'deduction' which is engaged in to derive the *shariah* ruling with regard to a particular matter when neither the Divine sources of the faith (*nass*) nor the consensus of the *ulema* (*ijma*) have made any explicit pronouncement on the issue at hand.

This is the sort of work that the *fuqaha* of the second Islamic century engaged in. Many new issues emerged during the Abbasid period, for which answers were not directly or explicitly mentioned in the Quran and the Sunnah. At this time, the *fuqaha* resorted to *ijtihad* to come up with answers to these questions, deriving them through deduction and analogy from the Quran and Sunnah. In this way, Muslims were able to acquire guidance from the *shariah* in the new contexts that they were faced with.

Things began to change, however, after the second or third Islamic century. Due to certain reasons, a wrong impression took root that whatever deduction or *ijtihad* from the Quran and Sunnah had to be made had already been fully completed by the earlier *fuqaha*, and that, henceforth, there was no need for this process to be carried further. It thus came to be believed that younger generations of Muslims had to simply study the books of these earlier *fuqaha*, and from these texts find *shariah* rules for new issues. In this way, the *fuqaha* of the Abbasid period were granted the status of *mujtahid-e mutlaq* or 'absolute' *mujtahids*, and those of later periods only that of *mujtahid-e muqayyad* or 'limited' *mujtahids*. The *ijtihad* of the *fuqaha* of the earlier period was based on the Quran and the Sunnah, but for the later *fuqaha ijtihad*, if at all allowed, was to be restricted within the framework and boundaries set by the views and the writings of the former, within which they were expected to engage in seeking to explicate *shariah* instructions.

Intellectual Dilemma

This is the starting point for the Muslims' intellectual dilemma that has continued unresolved for a long time. This misconception about *ijtihad* has led Muslim thought to stagnate. It rendered *ijtihad* extremely narrow and confined, leading to Muslim backwardness. *Ijtihad* is not something that can be chosen or rejected; rather, it is an indispensable and natural activity. Thus, to stop *ijtihad* is to seek to stop the progress of nature, and those who seek to do this cause the end of their own progress. The life of a river lies in its flow. If the waters of a river are blocked, it will no longer remain a river, and will turn into a stagnant pool. Likewise, if a community tries to stop *ijtihad*, it will completely stagnate and will fail to progress in material, religious, and spiritual terms.

The Capacity to Reassess

A *muqallid*, being a blind follower of past juridical opinions, remains stuck in his own groove, and is unable to reassess or re-think any issues on his own. He walks on only one familiar path, even if this leads him nowhere. In contrast, a person characterised by an *ijtihadi* mindset constantly examines issues, past and present, and, accordingly, charts his path. The taqlidi mind is stuck in the past, while the *ijtihadi* mind is geared to the future.

A good illustration of this is provided in Indian history. When, from the late eighteenth century onwards, India came under British control, Muslim leaders had, largely, only one aim in mind: to engage the British in a military fight. Their minds were moulded by the old perceptions of war and conflict and the notion of *dar ul-harb* ('abode of war'), and that is why they could only think of fighting the British and destroying them. It was this perception that led Tipu Sultan into battle with British forces in 1799, the outcome of which was that he himself was killed in the battlefield, bringing his vast empire to an abrupt and violent end. It was the same vision that was behind the launching of a violent uprising against the British by Muslim leaders in 1857. Similar revolts occurred even after that, throughout the nineteenth century. The outcome of these violent movements was the same: widespread loss and destruction that Muslims had to suffer. No benefit accrued from these to Islam or to the Muslims.

This was the case with those people who, in the matter concerning the British, adopted a *taqlidi* approach. At the same time, history affords us with an example of a Muslim leader who adopted an *ijtihadi* approach on the same matter and in the same period. This person was the renowned Egyptian Islamic scholar, Syed Muhammad

Rashid Riza (d.1935). He visited Lucknow in 1912 at the invitation of Maulana Shibli Numani to attend a convention at the Dar ul-Ulum Nadwat ul-Ulema. Thereafter, he went to the Dar ul-Ulum at Deoband, which at that time was, in a sense, the centre of an anti-British Muslim movement. A special function was organised there for him, and as he addressed the crowd he said:

> [One] aspect of the spread of Islam has to do with non-Muslims. There are numerous different sorts of idol worshippers in India, people who worship trees, the moon, the sun, the stars and even those who revere bad things. If Muslims had a set of committed missionaries they could tell these people about Islam, and we could gain considerably more success than Christian missionaries. In addition, every far-sighted Muslim must note that Muslims are much less in number than non-Muslims in this country, which makes them a vulnerable minority. The British Government, which is based on reason and justice, has established a balance between non-Muslims and Muslims. If, God forbid, this balance should ever be destroyed, the Indian Muslims might even face the same fate as that of their co-religionists in Spain. That is why there must be among us a group whose task it should be to combat misconceptions about Islam that now abound. This is really very essential. But, this is not possible without knowledge of modern philosophy. Hence, this group of Islamic missionaries must be familiar with the issues and concerns of modern philosophy.
>
> This speech of Syed Muhammad Rashid Riza is an example of ijtihadi insight. On closely examining the then prevailing conditions, he well understood that the balance in pre-Partition India between Muslims and the non-Muslim majority was

because of the existence of a third party: the British. He also
knew that when this third party withdrew, the balance would be
suddenly destroyed, after which the situation for Muslims would
be totally transformed, and that political independence would
not end their problems and instead only create new ones.

On the basis of this insight, Syed Muhammad Rashid Riza advised
Indian Muslim leaders to be active in the field of *da'wah* or inviting
others to the faith of Islam, rather than engaging in war and conflict.
He suggested that instead of making preparations for war, they should
make intellectual preparations so that they could effectively engage in
missionary work, and to do so according to the needs of the times.
However, the then Muslim leaders were drowning deeply in anti-British
hatred that they could not even imagine that it would be possible
for them to engage in any sort of constructive work as long as the
British remained in India. Thus, a great historical opportunity was
lost, and the only reason for this was the lack of *ijtihadi* insight.

This is just one example among many of how, because of the
lack of *ijtihad* and continued adherence to *taqlid*, Muslims have had
to undergo much unnecessary suffering and damage, causing them
to further stagnate.

The Development of *Fiqh* in the Period of Muslim Political Dominance

The Sunni Muslim corpus of *fiqh* was compiled mainly in the
Abbasid period, which was a time when Muslims were the most
powerful political force in the world. Naturally, therefore, this *fiqh*
was influenced by the mentality of this age of Muslim political
domination. Because of this, it turned into a sort of what can be
called jurisprudence of dominance.

I once happened to listen to a speech by a famous Islamic scholar. The title of his lecture was 'Islam in the Modern Age'. At the end of the lecture, a man from the audience asked the scholar what he felt was the guidance that the *shariah* provided in relation to a country like India. The scholar stood silent for a while, and then answered that it was very difficult to respond to this question. The reason, he said, was that the Islamic *shariah* presented a model based on Muslim political dominance but had no such model based on a position of modesty or lack of Muslim political dominance.

For a long time, the question kept turning in my mind as to why this scholar had not been able to find a model based on a position of modesty for Muslims. Finally, I discovered that this scholar, like many other contemporary Muslim leaders, erroneously viewed the corpus of medieval *fiqh* as synonymous with the Islamic shariah. This *fiqh* was developed at the time when Muslims were a dominant political power, and so whether consciously or otherwise, it had turned into a *fiqh* of the political dominant. It thus represented the condition and context of Muslim political power. This is why when, in the modern period Muslims lost political power, they felt that the *shariah* was unable to provide them with proper guidance. Because of this, they assumed that their main task should be to again acquire political power, for which they felt the need to unleash wars against others.

It is true that the corpus of *fiqh* which was developed in the period of Muslim political domination did not provide appropriate guidance for Muslims living in a position of modesty or lack of political domination. Undoubtedly, however, the Quran does provide this sort of guidance. After all, the Quran provides guidance for all conditions and contexts, including where Muslims are not a politically dominant community. God knew that Muslims shall not always enjoy the same position forever, but instead, would be faced with different situations including being either politically dominant or bereft of political power. Even the Prophet Muhammad faced both these situations. In the period of his prophethood in Mecca, the Muslims were in a position of modesty, lacking political domination, while his period in Medina was one of political power. Both periods of the Prophet's life provide Muslims with appropriate models to emulate. Neither of these two models is superior or inferior to the other. God judges all actions according to their intentions, not according to external conditions, including political or non-political ones.

The Case of the Vilification of the Prophet

To understand this issue, consider the issue of the vilification of the Prophet. The *fuqaha* are almost entirely unanimous in claiming that the punishment for vilification of the Prophet, even if it is only through indirect indication, is death. Only very few *fuqaha* have opined otherwise. Even today, Muslim scholars approvingly quote this opinion of the *fuqaha* in their writings. Now, the question arises that if the *shariah* indeed lays down death for vilifying the Prophet, then why is it that this was not the punishment ordered for this crime in the early Islamic period?

Early Islamic history provides numerous instances of people who vilified the Prophet but yet were not killed for their act. A striking example in this regard is that of Abdullah bin Abu Ibn Sulul of Medina, who used to openly vilify the Prophet. Yet, and despite the insistence of his followers, the Prophet did not order that he should be killed. Instead, he died a natural death.

What was the reason for not ordering that he be killed? The noted Islamic scholar Ibn Taimiyyah argues that this was because the Prophet felt that if this man had been ordered to be slain people would have been repelled by Islam, because Islam was then in a 'weak' position.

In this regard, we should raise the question as to why there is this difference between the *fiqh* of the early Islamic period and that which developed soon after, in the Abbasid age, to which many Muslim clerics still cling today. To further explore this issue, consider the fatwa delivered by Ayatollah Khomeini of Iran in February 1989, opining that because Salman Rushdie had vilified the Prophet in his book *Satanic Verses*, it was obligatory on the part of Muslims to kill him. When this fatwa was issued, I was one of the very few Muslims who did not agree. Muslims organised massive demonstrations in many countries in support of the fatwa, but despite this, Salman Rushdie could not be killed. Furthermore, the fatwa and the massive Muslim support for it only gave Islam a bad name across the world, creating the wrong image of Islam as a barbaric religion.

In today's world, many people consider freedom of opinion to be the most important right for human beings. For some people, in fact, it is a substitute for religion. That is why many people saw Khomeini's fatwa as an assault on their religion or freedom and came out in full support of Rushdie. The global media also passionately defended him. Thus it came to be that the apprehension because of which the Prophet restrained from ordering the death of Abdullah bin Abu Ibn Sulul came true—and a thousand times more intensely—as a result of the fatwa against Rushdie.

Carefully examine these two opposite positions. The Prophet's action indicates that in a matter concerning vilification of the Prophet, no matter how severe it may be, the practical consequences of ordering the death of the criminal must be considered. If the followers of Islam do not have the sort of control on the situation to prevent the negative consequences of slaying the criminal, they should not inflict this punishment on him. Rather, they should leave the matter to God. But the opinion of the *fuqaha* is the opposite—that any and every person who vilifies the Prophet must be immediately killed.

In this context, the question must be asked as to why, in this matter, Muslims did not take guidance from the example of the Prophet but instead adhered to the contrary opinion of the *fuqaha* and, in doing so, demanded the death penalty for Rushdie. The answer to this question is that Muslims today continue to be wedded to the notion of *taqlid* of the medieval *fuqaha*. Many Muslim clerics believe that the doors of *ijtihad* directly from the Quran and Sunnah have been shut, and that they can only engage in very limited *ijtihad—ijtihad-e muqayyad*. In other words, they have been wrongly led to believe that Muslims can no longer derive answers to issues directly from the Quran and Sunnah. They feel that all they can do is to study the fatwas of the past *fuqaha* and blindly imitate them. This is why they adopted that particular stance in the Rushdie affair.

As discussed earlier, the present-day corpus of *fiqh* was compiled in a period when Muslims enjoyed political dominance. At that time, Muslims were in a position to effectively take down any stirrings of revolt. But today the conditions have changed; Muslims no longer have the same sort of political control. Moreover, they are faced with a number of unfavourable conditions. For instance, the belief that freedom of expression has no limits, that it is the be-all and end-all of everything, and the emergence of the mass media forever on the look-out for what it considers as 'hot news'. It was because of these new conditions that, despite the massive Muslim agitation, it was not possible to kill Rushdie. Moreover, as mentioned earlier, the Muslim response only resulted in Islam acquiring a bad name throughout the world. Many non-Muslims were led to believe that Islam is a barbaric religion that stirs up fanaticism among its followers. This was the result of seeking to follow and impose a *fiqh* prescription devised in the age of Muslim political domination in today's distinct context.

If, with regard to the Rushdie case, Muslims had adopted the method of *ijtihad-e mutlaq* or absolute *ijtihad* and, accordingly, had sought guidance directly from the Quran and Sunnah instead of engaging in *taqlid* of the past *fuqaha*, they would have realised that the right solution to the controversy was not to issue a fatwa calling for Rushdie's death, but rather, to abstain from any violent reaction and instead engage in peaceful *da'wah* work to explain the truth to the people about Islam and the Prophet. But because they remain stuck in the morass of the *fiqh* which had developed in the period of Muslim political dominance, they could only consider the solution that was argued for by the *fuqaha* of that period—death penalty for vilification of the Prophet. That, in turn, led to Islam wrongly getting a bad name the world over.

This is a translation of an excerpt from a chapter titled *Taqlid Aur Ijtihad* ('*Taqlid* and *Ijtihad*') in Maulana Wahiduddin Khan's book *Din-o-Shariat: Din-e Islam Ka Ek Fikri Muta'ala* ('Religion and the *Shariah*: An Intellectual Study of the Religion of Islam') Goodword Books, New Delhi, 2003, pp. 214–24.

13

Contextually Relevant *Ijtihad* and a Culture of Intellectual Critique

A religious scholar once dissented from his spiritual preceptor on a particular matter. Somebody rebuked him, saying that he had criticised his master. In reply, the scholar said, 'I love my teacher, but I love the truth even more'. This reply points to a very important truth—that when a dissenting opinion or critique is articulated on a particular matter, even if this concerns the view of a particular person, it must not be seen as a personal attack on someone, but rather, as an intellectual activity. This sort of criticism certainly involves a certain person, because without specifically mentioning this person and his views, criticism would simply be some languid expression of a certain counter viewpoint, and the basic objective of criticism would not be attained. Yet it should not be regarded as a personal attack on that individual.

Criticism or the expression of dissenting views was a characteristic feature of early Muslim history. The Companions of the Prophet differed with each other on numerous occasions, and they generally openly expressed these differences. Similarly, in the case of the first two generations of Muslims who succeeded the Companions, as well as the commentators on the Hadith and the early *ulema*. They did not consider this as bad or unworthy, nor did they try to stamp out criticism and differences. This was because they regarded this from the point of view of principle, and not as a personal attack on anyone.

To listen to criticism in a cool and dispassionate manner is proof that one is not immersed in a personality cult. It is evident that what is important for one is a principle, not a particular person. A true intellectual will accept the critique of an individual, including of himself or someone dear to him, but will not accept that a cherished principle be violated. This can only happen when the true spirit of religion is alive in a person. But when a community declines, people start blindly imitating certain supposed leaders and refuse to tolerate any criticism of them. They do not display the same zeal for defending principles as they do for defending these hallowed individuals. This is why they cannot tolerate criticism; when they are faced with any criticism of these leaders of theirs, they become enraged. This indicates that they are yet to reach the stage of the proper realisation of the Truth. They erroneously confuse some cherished individuals, and their views, with the Truth.

The Benefits of Criticism

To critique someone's views is not to abuse him or to unnecessarily find fault with him. Rather, this sort of intellectual critique is a blessing. It opens new doors of knowledge and uncovers new aspects and dimensions of various issues. It leads to intellectual sharing between the critic and the subject of the critique, and this equally benefits both and helps expand their intellectual horizons. Genuine critique is actually an intellectual gift that is presented by the critic to the person whose views he critiques. This is why the Caliph Umar asked for God to extend his mercy to those who presented him the gift of pointing out his faults.

It would not be an exaggeration to say that from childhood onwards I have always been in favour of criticism. Because of this, I have always wanted my friends to subject my views to intellectual critique. When a close companion of mine, Maulana Anis Luqman Nadwi, went to Arabia for the first time, he was asked by an Arab *shaikh* what work he did in India. He replied, 'I am the critic of India's greatest critic'. From this you can gauge how passionately I support intellectual criticism.

Intellectual exchange is the greatest experience that a true intellectual can have. In the process of intellectual criticism, a certain individual appears to be challenged, but in fact, it is not this individual as such, but rather, a certain issue that is the target or object of criticism. True intellectual criticism is a sort of discussion on a certain topic by two people even if it be in the context of discussing a particular person. True intellectual criticism is not to be regarded as a personal attack on someone's integrity, because it aims not at an individual *per se,* but rather at a view or set of views about a certain matter. If the critique is proper and sound, it enables a person to improve and to correct his or her stance.

Even if someone's critique of the views of a certain person is not proper or sound, it can still enable new facets of the issue under discussion to be uncovered. If a person whose views are critiqued is able to accept criticism, it can help advance his own intellect and help him think in a more creative way. It can enable him to express his own views in a more effective and convincing manner. In fact, intellectual criticism is always beneficial, even if the critique may not be valid.

In this regard, let me refer to a personal instance. In 1960, when I was in Lucknow, I met a certain non-Muslim scholar. He was an atheist. In the course of our conversation, he criticised the Prophet Muhammad. He also mockingly asked what difference it would make if the Prophet were to be removed from history. Undoubtedly, his words were very provocative. Had I got angry with him, all I could have done was to lose my temper and leave. But, by the grace of God, I maintained my emotional balance. I was able to think about what had transpired in a positive manner, and then replied that if the Prophet were to be removed from history, mankind would be in the same position that it was in before the Prophet's advent. Thereafter, this conversation and criticism forced me to ponder on the life of the Prophet, including on aspects of it that had not been clear to me before. In this way, this scholar's criticism became for me a means to discover dimensions of the Prophet's life that I had not seriously thought of earlier. I started seriously studying the issue and a result of that was my book *Islam, The Creator of the Modern Age*. This is an example to show that if one listens to criticism and does not get agitated or angry, but instead maintains one's balance, it can prove to be of immense benefit.

Right and Wrong Criteria

The *taqlidi* approach leads to numerous difficulties and problems. Perhaps the biggest damage that it causes is that it makes people seek to understand the truth not on the basis of the truth itself, but rather, through the views of some supposedly learned elder of theirs. For those who strictly abide by *taqlid*, the views of such supposedly learned elders become the criterion of truth and they are considered to be sources of emulation. They strictly refuse to listen to any person other than such supposed elders, no matter how valid that person's argument may be. This was one of the major reasons why, in every age, prophets were rejected by people. The prophets appeared to the people whom they addressed as different, quite in contrast to the elders whom they believed they should follow, and so they did not respect them. When the prophets critiqued the persons whom they held in high regard, they grew even more agitated and were unwilling to listen to what they had to say.

The biggest difference between the *ijtihadi* and *taqlidi* mindset is that those who sternly abide by *taqlid* seek to understand the truth solely on the basis of the views of certain chosen elders of theirs, while those who stand by *ijtihad* seek to understand the truth on the basis of proof, rather than on the basis of the views of certain personalities. This is why the former are bereft of the faith that is based on a deep understanding and realisation, which is the highest form of faith. The font of such faith is self-discovery. Those with a *taqlidi* mindset do not freely use their intellect, and that is why they fail to recognise the sort of faith that is based on deep understanding and realisation.

The opposite is true for those with an *ijtihadi* mindset. The windows of the minds of such people are always open, and they are always ready to ponder and think freely. If anything appears to them as true, they immediately recognise and accept it.

The most important thing for human beings is to discern and realise the truth. To discover the truth is surely the greatest blessing that one can enjoy. But this great blessing can be had only by those with an *ijtihadi* mindset. Those who are lost in the darkness caused by stagnant *taqlidi* thought can never experience the truth that is based on genuine understanding.

Need for a Revolutionary Mindset

In his book *Aqd al-Jayyad*, the noted Indian scholar Shah Waliullah (d.1762) discusses issues related to *taqlid* and *ijtihad* in considerable detail. He writes that a *mujtahid* is one who possesses five forms of knowledge: that of the Quran or the Book of God; of the Sunnah of the Prophet; of the sayings of the early *ulema*; of the relevant languages; and of the principles of analogy and derivation or *istinbat*. Now, the conditions that Shah Waliullah and other *ulema* like him laid down for a *mujtahid* are in themselves correct, but these apply only to 'restricted' or *muqayyad ijtihad*, and are inadequate for *ijtihad* which is not 'restricted'.

Ijtihad is of two types: the first is the 'ordinary' or *'am* sort of *ijtihad*, and the other is 'special' or *khas ijtihad*. The 'ordinary' *ijtihad* is that kind of *ijtihad* that is related to external conditions (*ahwal-e zahiri*). On the other hand, 'special' *ijtihad* relates to underlying or non-apparent conditions (*ahwal-e batini*)—that is to say, those conditions that are not visible externally but are present as a powerful undercurrent. The difference between the two can be expressed in another way, by saying that 'ordinary' *ijtihad* relates to external eyesight (*basarat*), while 'special' *ijtihad* relates to insight (*basirat*).

For instance, for an issue such as whether one's ablutions before prayers are valid if one is wearing factory-made socks and wipes them with one's hands or if they are nullified if one takes an injection, a *mujtahid* can rely on the five forms of knowledge that Shah Waliullah mentions. For this purpose, one can also draw analogies from the opinions expressed by the earlier *ulema* on similar issues.

But for 'special' *ijtihad*, one needs another form of knowledge in addition to these five, and this is what is referred to in a *hadith* report, according to which it is binding on a wise person that he should have knowledge of his times. Thus, a *mujtahid* must have a deep understanding of his society and his age in order to engage in proper *ijtihad*, in addition to possessing the five forms of traditional knowledge mentioned above. This additional knowledge can be acquired only through further study and a careful pondering and reflection on reality.

Early Islamic history is replete with examples of such forms of creative *ijtihad*. One such instance was that represented by the Treaty of Hudaibiyah. The terms of the treaty appeared, on the face of it, to be loaded against the Muslims, because this ten-year no-war pact was based on the acceptance of the terms set by their opponents. Because of this, many Companions of the Prophet found it difficult to accept the treaty, so much so that Umar Farooq labelled it as an insult. But the truth about the whole affair was revealed in the Quran, when it said, 'For He [God] knew what ye knew not, and He granted besides this, a speedy victory' (*Surah Al-Fatah*: 27). This meant that the reality of the matter was different from what it appeared to be, the truth of which God knew and on the basis of which He instructed His Prophet to enter into this Treaty.

The Treaty, as I said, appeared to be based on the one-sided conditions of the Muslims' opponents. But the underlying truth, which did not appear to those who could not fathom it, was that it would do away with the state of war between Muslims and their opponents that had blocked interaction between them. It would enable them to meet and interact with each other, and thereby, promote an open dialogue between them. In the course of this, others would be able to recognise the beauty of Islam, and finally, what the Quran refers to when it says 'And thou dost see the people enter Allah's Religion in crowds' (*Surah An-Nasr*: 2) would take place.

This is precisely what happened. At the time of the Treaty of Hudaibiyah, Muslims numbered less than 1,500, but in the period of peace that followed the Treaty, Islam rapidly spread, and in less than two years the number of Muslims grew to around ten thousand and Muslims acquired power without resorting to war.

The same sort of thing happened in the thirteenth century, when much of the Muslim world was overrun by the marauding Tartars. They destroyed many Muslim cities and put a violent end to the Abbasid Caliphate. Many Muslims at that time believed that the Tartars could never be defeated. Yet although the Tartars had powerful weapons of war, they lacked a suitable ideology or world-view. In the course of interacting with Muslims, they learned about Islam. As they did not have any suitable ideology that could reply to it, they began converting *en masse* to Islam, and thus it was that, as the noted Orientalist scholar Philip K. Hitti put it, 'The religion of Muslims [...] conquered where their arms had failed'.

Now, turn to developments in later periods of history. Take the example of Shah Waliullah. In his time, the Mughal Empire in India had started weakening, showing signs of a rapid and complete collapse. Shah Waliullah strove to strengthen this Muslim dynasty, and sent off letters to various Muslim rulers asking them to wage wars with its enemies. He also advised the ruler of Kabul, Ahmad Shah Abdali, to invade India and vanquish the Sikhs and Marathas so that the Mughal Empire could be salvaged and strengthened.

This effort of Shah Waliullah is evidence of the fact that he looked only at the external conditions around him. He was totally unaware of the new flood of developments at the global level, in particular the stirrings of democracy that had by then begun making themselves felt. Shah Waliullah believed that he was the 'Support of the Age' or *qa'im uz-zaman*, and his entire thought process operated in the framework set by the Age of Monarchy. He had no idea what the coming Age of Democracy would mean. In the monarchical age, a single man controlled all levers of power, while democracy is based on the rule of the majority of the people. If Shah Waliullah had properly studied and understood the changing times that he was faced with, he would have focussed all his energies on the propagation of the faith in order to win over the majority of people. And, in this way, even if the Mughal Empire came to an end, the Muslims would still be able to maintain their power because of being in the majority. However, Shah Waliullah was completely unaware of the revolutionary importance of *da'wah* or inviting others to the faith. One indication of this is that his most famous book, *Hujjat Allah al-Balagha,* contains chapters on various issues and subjects but not even one on *da'wah.*

Take also the example of Syed Jamaluddin Afghani (d.1897). By his time, the British and the French had established their political domination over most of the Muslim world. Syed Jamaluddin Afghani spent his entire life struggling to end this domination. His slogan was, 'The East is for the People of the East'. On the surface, it appears today that Western domination has come to an end, for some sixty independent Muslim countries have appeared on the map of the world. However, in actual terms, conditions have not really changed. Muslim communities are still compelled to live under the domination of Western powers. This shows that Syed Jamaluddin Afghani could only see the external aspects of conditions around him, and not the various underlying processes and forces. Accordingly, he saw British and French domination of Muslim lands only in terms of their externally visible political control. This domination was a result of the West having acquired intellectual superiority in the fields of science and technology. But because of his medieval or *taqlidi* political mindset, Syed Jamaluddin Afghani could not properly appreciate this fact. Had he understood the importance of knowledge in the modern age, he might have viewed foreign political domination as only a temporary situation, and focussed his energies on the intellectual development of Muslims so that they could excel in the fields of science and technology. If he and his companions had abandoned the useless path of political jihad, and instead launched an intellectual jihad, the history of Muslim countries today would have been very different.

These examples should suffice to indicate that while the traditional five disciplines that Shah Waliullah and other *ulema* have outlined may be adequate for 'restricted' *ijtihad,* one more condition is necessary for 'absolute' or *mutlaq ijtihad:* a deep understanding of the conditions of the contemporary world. Without this there can be no effective *ijtihad* that can provide proper guidance to the community.

This is a translation of an excerpt from a chapter titled *Taqlid Aur Ijtihad* ('*Taqlid* and *Ijtihad*') in Maulana Wahiduddin Khan's book *Din-o-Shariat: Din-e Islam Ka Ek Fikri Muta'ala* ('Religion and the *Shariah*: An Intellectual Study of the Religion of Islam'), Goodword Books, New Delhi, 2003, pp. 240–50.

14

Taqlid, Ijtihad, and Democracy

In the wake of the Industrial Revolution in Europe, Western countries established their political and cultural domination over much of the rest of the world, leading to the emergence of European colonial empires. This posed a new and major challenge for Muslims. At that time, numerous Muslim leaders in various countries emerged, inspired to pursue a sole mission—to engage in armed jihad—thinking this to be the only solution to the challenge of Western imperialism. Despite two hundred years of armed struggle against the West, however, Muslims have not made substantial gains.

If this problem is examined in the light of the Quran and Hadith, it is clear that the solution lay somewhere else—in peaceful *da'wah* or missionary work. The Prophet was faced with a similar predicament, and the Quran's instruction to him in this context was to present the message of God to the people, for this would be the guarantee of his protection (*Surah Al-Maidah*: 67). The Quran advises us to engage in *da'wah* and propagation of Islam with wisdom (*hikmat*), and it adds that the result of this would be that one's foes would become one's friends. Thus, it declares:

> *And O Prophet, goodness and evil are not equal. Repel evil with what is best. You will see that he with whom you had enmity has become your closest friend (Surah Fussilat: 34).*

It would not be wrong to say that the Quran indicates that *da'wah* is the only solution. Why is it, then, that modern-day Muslims could not understand this? Why did they take to jihad, in the sense of physical warfare or *qital*, instead of *da'wah*, especially when it was not difficult to realise that in the given conditions, violence would cause nothing else than even more destruction for Muslims? Why is it that modern-day Muslim leaders made such a terrible blunder by claiming that violent jihad was the only solution?

In my opinion, one of the main reasons for this was that these leaders considered that *ijtihad-e mutlaq* or *ijtihad* involving direct and unrestricted derivation of rules from the Quran and Hadith to be prohibited to them. In accordance with their deeply-rooted *taqlidi* mentality, they believed that they had to strictly follow the guidance and rules of the established corpus of *fiqh*. Now, these books of *fiqh* were full of rules and commandments about jihad, in the sense of *qital*. In contrast, they hardly contained any rules that could provide guidance for the task of *da'wah*. They had long and detailed chapters on jihad, in the sense of *qital*, but none at all on *da'wah* and *tabligh*.

These leaders could have learned about the need to engage in *da'wah* as stressed in the Quran, but they viewed the Quran simply as a book of laws. For rules for new issues they turned not to the

Quran, but instead, to the established corpus of *fiqh*, which, as I said, does not contain any guidance for *da'wah* work. From this it can be gauged how useful and essential *ijtihad*, in the sense of directly deriving rules from the Quran and Hadith, is—and contrarily--how harmful *taqlid* can be, with respect to the established corpus of *fiqh*, considering it as the sole source of rules.

This same mistake was made by many Indian Muslim leaders who, in the wake of the establishment of British rule, declared India to be *dar ul-harb* or 'abode of war'. In 1823, the scholar Shah Abdul Aziz of Delhi issued a fatwa, opining that India had now turned into *dar ul-harb*. Thereafter, 500 Indian *ulema* signed a fatwa claiming that it had now become obligatory for the Indian Muslims to engage in jihad, in the sense of *qital*, against the British. Consequently, many Muslims began getting involved in violent anti-British activities, thinking this to be their religious duty. This carried on for over a hundred years but it proved to be completely fruitless. Despite this, it is shocking to see how some Muslims still believe—and there are those among them who even openly announce—that India today is still *dar ul-harb* and that they can solve their problems through armed jihad.

The reason for this peculiar situation is that the minds of these people are still stuck in the groove of the traditional corpus of *fiqh* based on the established *maslaks*, or schools of thought, whose views on *taqlid* and *ijtihad* they consider themselves duty-bound to follow. According to this tradition of medieval *fiqh*, countries like India are categorised as *dar ul-harb*. Had these Muslim leaders gone back, even before the formation of the schools of *fiqh*, directly to the Quran and Sunnah, they would undoubtedly have realised that the status of a country like India is not that of *dar ul-harb*, but rather, that of what can be called *dar ul-da'wah* or 'abode of missionary work'. But this they did not do because they considered *ijtihad*, in the sense of directly approaching the Quran and Sunnah to derive rules, to be prohibited to them. In accordance with their *taqlidi* approach, they limited themselves wholly to the corpus of established *fiqh* for guidance. As is known, this corpus of *fiqh* speaks in detail about *dar ul-harb*, but not at all about *dar ul-da'wah*.

Present-Day *Fiqh* Is Inadequate

The present corpus of *fiqh* was compiled by the second or third Islamic centuries. Many Muslims erroneously believe that this *fiqh* is complete and that it contains all the teachings of the Quran and Hadith related to human life. This reflects the belief that, following the compilation of this corpus of *fiqh*, the doors of *ijtihad-e mutlaq* or 'absolute' *ijtihad* were fully closed. According to such thinking, therefore, only *ijtihad-e muqayyad* or *ijtihad* within the established schools of *fiqh*—or what can be called *taqlidi ijtihad*—is now permissible, if at all.

This belief might have been seen as appropriate in the past, but when social conditions began to undergo massive changes with the passing of the traditional age and the advent of modern science, it proved to be extremely harmful for Muslims. Muslims had come to view the corpus of *fiqh* as a complete legal system, and believed that there was no need to look beyond it for solutions to all their problems. Because of this, modern-day Muslims were unable to access guidance on numerous issues which was present in the Quran and Sunnah, but not in the established corpus of *fiqh*.

Let me point to an instance in this regard. The political revolutions that accompanied the advent of the modern age brought about Democracy as a new political system. The corpus of *fiqh* had been developed in a prior age, that of Monarchy. That is why it had no conception of modern Democracy. Consequently, Muslims who thought in terms of the established corpus of *fiqh* could not appreciate or understand the importance of Democracy. This explains why some of them branded it as irreligious (*la-dini*), even 'prohibited' (*haram*). Others denounced it as a system of counting heads, where numbers are given the importance that quality deserves.

In fact, Democracy has the potential of being a great blessing for Muslims. In contrast to the old monarchical system, Democracy is based on the principle of power-sharing. It offers Muslims the opportunity to gain political importance if they act wisely. But, once again, Muslims failed to do so because of their lack of *ijtihadi* insight. Instead, their *taqlidi* approach led them to talk about such bizarre plans as launching a movement to establish the Caliphate in America and to change the name of California to *Caliph-ornia*, and dreaming up similar laughable schemes. They failed to see how they might be able to make a place for themselves in democratic countries by participating in democratic governance and getting involved in democratic processes.

The reason for this terrible backwardness of present-day Muslim thought is the refusal to engage in *ijtihad*, to come out of the boundaries of the established corpus of *fiqh* and gain guidance directly from the Quran and Hadith. Muslims should ponder on the Quran directly, for this can provide them appropriate guidance in this regard. The Quran says that at the time of the Prophet Joseph, Egypt was ruled by a certain king who, although a polytheist or *mushrik*, appointed Joseph to a high political position. He was made in-charge of food and agriculture, but he had more powers than this, acting, in a sense, as the deputy of the king, because in the agricultural age, the economy of countries was based essentially on agriculture. In other words, Joseph's position in the political system was equivalent to that of the highest official.

If modern-day Muslims did not bind themselves to *taqlid,* but instead approached the Quran in a spirit of *ijtihad* and pondered on it carefully, they would have realised that this incident about Joseph is a prophetic example for them to seek to emulate. They could have understood that they could use the principle of power-sharing of modern Democracy for their benefit, being confident that doing so is in accordance with a prophetic practice.

This is a translation of an excerpt from a chapter titled *Taqlid Aur Ijtihad* ('*Taqlid* and *Ijtihad*') in Maulana Wahiduddin Khan's book *Din-o-Shariat: Din-e Islam Ka Ek Fikri Muta'ala* ('Religion and the *Shariah*: An Intellectual Study of the Religion of Islam'), Goodword Books, New Delhi, 2003, pp. 224–228.

15
Taqlidi Vs. *Ijtihadi* Approaches

Human minds can be categorised into two types: *taqlidi*, or stagnant and imitative of past precedent, and *ijtihadi*, or dynamic and creative. The former denotes closed-mindedness; the latter, its opposite, or open-mindedness. The *taqlidi* mind attains a certain level and then stagnates, while the *ijtihadi* mind keeps travelling ahead, stopping only at death.

The difference between the *taqlidi* and the *ijtihadi* mindsets can be illustrated with the help of an example. William Shakespeare was a famous English writer, and so was George Bernard Shaw, who was born some two hundred and fifty years after the death of the former. Shaw's contribution to English literature was less than that of Shakespeare, and he himself admitted this when he said, 'I am smaller in stature than Shakespeare, but I stand upon his shoulders'. This is an example of an *ijtihadi* way of thinking. A society characterised by such persons constantly progresses in terms of thought and intellect. Each new generation in such a society builds on the contributions of its predecessors, adds to them, and then transmits this legacy to the generations that come after it. But contemporary Muslim societies present a completely different picture. In modern times, their intellectual development has come to an almost complete halt. This is because they have developed a *taqlidi*, as opposed to *ijtihadi*, way of thinking, and consider *ijtihad* to be almost a sin. Many Muslims mistakenly believe that in terms of religious perspectives, the *ulema* of the past have accomplished all that there was to, and that today our task is simply to study the books that they wrote and strictly follow them.

This approach is a major hurdle in the path of our intellectual progress. In this regard, Muslims can adopt one of two positions: to recognise, like Shaw did with regard to Shakespeare, that their stature might be less than that of the *ulema* of the past, but despite this, they are standing on the latter's shoulders; or to believe that because their stature is less than that of the *ulema* of the past, they must remain forever at the latter's feet.

The first of these two approaches represents an *ijtihadi* way of thinking, which is conducive to constant intellectual development. In a society characterised by such an approach, each new generation fully respects those that went before it and, building on their contributions, makes even more progress. In contrast, the second approach represents a *taqlidi* way of thinking, which keeps Muslim thought stagnant, preventing it from moving in the direction of the constantly progressing stages of knowledge and understanding that Islam stands for. It also causes Muslims to fall behind other communities in the intellectual field, killing their intellectual faculties.

Let me elaborate on this point with the help of a *hadith* report. Once, in Medina, when a procession carrying a dead body for burial passed by the Prophet, he stood up, out of respect, on seeing it. When it was pointed out to him that the deceased was a Jew, he simply remarked that the man was a human being.

This incident is included in his collection of Hadith by Imam Bukhari, who made an immense contribution to Hadith studies by collecting over 7,000 reports that he considered authentic from several hundred thousand reports that had been attributed to the Prophet. He mentioned this *hadith* in the chapter on burial in his *Sahih al-Bukhari*. If we were to adopt a *taqlidi* approach and consider this *hadith* simply as something related to burial, and not more than just that, we would not be able to learn anything new from this *hadith*. We would simply parrot what the earlier commentators on Hadith have said about it, without being able to derive anything new from it. While we respect the intellectual contributions of the earlier exegetes of Hadith, we cannot accept all that they have written as gospel truth. Many *ulema* of the past have commented on this *hadith* report, offering various theories for the Prophet's action. Some of them claim that this practice of standing up when the corpse of a non-Muslim passed by was later abrogated, or that the Prophet stood up because he did not want the corpse of a Jew to be at a level higher than that of his head. Still other explanations have been given, all of them based on personal speculation and lacking in adequate proof. This *hadith* narrative very clearly indicates that the Prophet stood up out of respect for the dead man, and not because of any of the reasons that these Hadith commentators had suggested. In other words, this *hadith* is not simply about burial, as those with a *taqlidi* mindset would imagine. Rather, it is a fine example of respect for humankind, irrespective of religion, as those with an *ijtihadi* mindset might be able to discover. It could be offered as a counter to those who claim that while Islam preaches respect for fellow Muslims, it does not do so with regard to people of other faiths. This *hadith*, if approached in an *ijtihadi* way, can be presented as evidence of the Islamic principle that all human beings are worthy of respect, no matter what their religion or community. On the other hand, if this *hadith* is approached in a taqlidi fashion and interpreted in the same way as those traditionalist commentators have done, this vital Islamic principle will be completely occluded.

Consideration for Context

According to a report also contained in the *Sahih al-Bukhari*, the Prophet told his wife Ayesha that when the Quraish rebuilt the Ka'aba in Mecca they did not do so on its original foundation as set by the Prophet Abraham, but had changed it. Hearing this, Ayesha asked the Prophet why he could not restructure the Ka'aba on its original foundation. To this the Prophet replied that the Quraish had only then recently renounced infidelity for Islam, and it was possible that if he were to do so, it might cause them to agitate. He added that had there been no danger of this happening he would certainly have done what Ayesha had suggested.

Imam Bukhari has included this *hadith* in his chapter on Haj. If we were to consider the *hadith* simply in this way, reflecting a *taqlidi* approach, all that we would gain would be some information about the glories of Mecca. If, on the other hand, we adopt an *ijtihadi* approach to view this *hadith*, we can gain a new understanding of what can be called the wisdom of practical living. To leave the Ka'aba on the foundations laid by the Quraish, instead of reconstructing it on the foundation laid by the Prophet Abraham, might appear to have been incorrect. Despite this, the Prophet chose not to reconstruct it in the latter way because in the given circumstances this would have posed additional problems.

From this practice of the Prophet we can derive the principle that in life, when sometimes faced with certain challenges, for the moment we should look not at what is right and what is wrong, but instead, at what is possible and what is not.

Abiding by this principle is a key to succeeding in this world. In today's world, many of the failures of Muslims have been brought about by their refusal to abide by this principle. They did not look at problems or challenges from the point of view of what is possible and what is not, but rather, considered them only from the perspective of what they thought was right and what was not. Accordingly, they rushed into action, hoping to attain what they thought was ideal, although, in the given circumstances, achieving this was not actually possible. Many of the sacrifices that modern-day Muslims have made but have not borne any fruits were a result of abandoning this principle referred to by this *hadith*. The major cause of this attitude is the *taqlidi* mindset.

Gradualism in Establishing Islamic Commandments

According to another *hadith* report in the *Sahih al-Bukhari*, Ayesha once mentioned that many of the earliest chapters of the Quran that were revealed dealt with the subject of heaven and hell and that only after people's faith in Islam had become firm that verses dealing with issues that are permissible (*halal*) and forbidden (*haram*) were set down. She added that had the commandments forbidding adultery and the consumption of alcohol been revealed in the beginning, instead of later, people would have refused to obey them.

Imam Bukhari has included this *hadith* in his chapter on the compilation of the Quran. If, in accordance with a *taqlidi* perspective, we were to view this *hadith* simply from the point of view of it being related to the compilation of the Quran, we would not be able to derive any other knowledge from it. On the other hand, by engaging in *ijtihad*, reflecting on the wider implications of this *hadith* and going beyond its relation to the question of the compilation of the Quran, we can discover that this *hadith* suggests a very important Islamic principle—that with regard to the enforcement or establishment of the rules of the shariah, a certain wisdom is required. It must be a gradual process, as it was in early Islamic times. Accordingly, at first peoples' faith was made firm so that they would be receptive to obeying Divine commands, and only after that were various laws introduced.

If the approach of present-day Islamic leaders is examined from this way of understanding this particular *hadith*, it appears that they have failed to appreciate the underlying broader implications of this *hadith* as regards the process of establishing Islamic laws in society. In many Muslim countries today, numerous movements and groups are demanding the enforcement of the *shariah*, but despite their many sacrifices, this has not happened anywhere, in the true sense of the term. This is because the faith of the Muslims has weakened, and their intellectual and emotional commitment has declined, which means that many of them are no longer willing to accept *shariah* laws. Despite their fervent attempts to enforce *shariah* laws, these Muslim leaders lacked the necessary *ijtihadi* approach and insight. They rushed into the political realm armed with their *taqlidi* baggage and so failed to achieve their objectives. They sought to impose *shariah* laws on society without first seeking to prepare society to willingly accept them, in contrast to what this *hadith* suggests is the right way.

Change in Field of Activity

According to another *hadith* report contained in the *Sahih al-Bukhari*, the Prophet is said to have remarked that he had been instructed to proceed to another town, Medina, which people referred to as Yathrib. Imam Bukhari has included this *hadith* in his chapter on the glories of Medina. Now, those with a *taqlidi* approach will view this *hadith* as providing information simply about the glories of Medina, and indeed, this is precisely what most exegetes of Hadith in the past have done. Some have even seen this *hadith* as indicating that to refer to Medina as Yathrib is disapproved of or *makruh*. However, the Quran itself refers to Medina as Yathrib, and so this explanation of this *hadith* is incorrect. But if one goes beyond the blind imitation of the past exegetes and ponders on this *hadith* from an *ijtihadi* perspective, one learns that it speaks about a very important Islamic principle—that of changing one's field or arena of action when the need so arises. This *hadith* indicates that when conditions became extremely severe and harsh for Muslims in Mecca, God commanded the Prophet to shift from there to another town, Yathrib, where he and his followers would find a more conducive atmosphere, so much so that it would emerge as a centre of Islam and people would start referring to it as the 'City of the Prophet' or *Madinat al-Rasul* or the 'City of Islam' or *Madinat al-Islam*.

This principle of shifting one's arena of activity if conditions so demand, which this *hadith* refers to, is important for success in various matters. It indicates that, if in a certain place, conditions are inappropriate one should shift to another place, or that if conflict would prove useless, one should seek to achieve one's objectives through peaceful dialogue. Unfortunately, today's Muslim leaders, burdened by their *taqlidi* mentality, have not been able to appreciate and act on this wisdom, because of which they have themselves faced considerable damage and loss. For instance, in several countries today, violent movements are engaged in conflict in the name of Islam, which have resulted in Muslims having to suffer massive loss of life and property. Because of their *taqlidi* approach, the leaders of these movements have been unable to appreciate the underlying message of this *hadith* of the Prophet. They would have been able understand the import of this *hadith* if they had an *ijtihadi* approach. In that case, and in accordance with the principle enunciated by this *hadith*, they would have abandoned the path of conflict and adopted peaceful means instead. Then, in accordance with the law of nature, they would have succeeded.

From these examples, I have sought to clarify the distinction between the *taqlidi* and *ijtihadi* approaches. The former stops at the initial stage and refuses to move ahead. In contrast, the latter proceeds through all the stages, seeking to reach the end. The first step is the end in itself for those who abide by *taqlid*, but for those inspired by and committed to *ijtihad*, it is only a means, a path to the higher stages. The relevance of this argument is obvious in the context of discussions about Islam, peace, and violence, as well as relations between Muslims and people of other faiths.

*This is a translation of an excerpt from a chapter titled *Taqlid Aur Ijtihad* ('*Taqlid* and *Ijtihad*') in Maulana Wahiduddin Khan's book *Din-o-Shariat: Din-e Islam Ka Ek Fikri Muta'ala* ('Religion and the *Shariah*: An Intellectual Study of the Religion of Islam') Goodword Books, New Delhi, 2003, pp. 204–14.